Universal Love

Surrendering to the God of Peace

JOHN DEAR

ORBIS BOOKS

Maryknoll, New York 10545

Founded in 1970, Orbis Books endeavors to publish works that enlighten the mind, nourish the spirit, and challenge the conscience. The publishing arm of the Maryknoll Fathers and Brothers, Orbis seeks to explore the global dimensions of the Christian faith and mission, to invite dialogue with diverse cultures and religious traditions, and to serve the cause of reconciliation and peace. The books published reflect the views of their authors and do not represent the official position of the Maryknoll Society. To learn more about Maryknoll and Orbis Books, please visit our website at www.orbisbooks.com.

Manufactured in the United States of America.

Manuscript editing and typesetting by Joan Weber Laflamme.

Library of Congress Cataloging-in-Publication Data

Names: Dear, John, 1959– author
Title: Universal love : surrendering to the God of peace / John Dear.
Description: Maryknoll, NY : Orbis Books, [2025] | Includes bibliographical references. | Summary: "How to live a life of peace and nonviolence by surrendering every day to God, or Universal Life"— Provided by publisher.
Identifiers: LCCN 2025035073 (print) | LCCN 2025035074 (ebook) | ISBN 9781626986510 trade paperback | ISBN 9798888661055 epub
Subjects: LCSH: Love—Religious aspects—Christianity | Peace of mind—Religious aspects—Christianity
Classification: LCC BV4639 .D353 2026 (print) | LCC BV4639 (ebook)
LC record available at https://lccn.loc.gov/2025035073
LC ebook record available at https://lccn.loc.gov/2025035074

Universal Love

For Chris and Danny,
Friends and Peacemakers

WE CAN ONLY learn to know ourselves and do what we can—namely surrender our will and fulfill God's will in us.

—St. Teresa of Ávila

EVERYBODY SURRENDERS TO something. If you don't surrender to God, don't think you don't surrender.

—E. Stanley Jones

SURRENDER WILL ALWAYS feel like dying, and yet it is the necessary path to liberation.

—Richard Rohr

I SHOULD KNOW by this time that just because I feel that everything is useless and going to pieces and badly done and futile, it is not really that way at all. Everything is all right. It is in the hands of God. Let us abandon everything to Divine Providence.

—Dorothy Day

DON'T LOOK FOR peace. The moment you completely accept your non-peace, your non-peace becomes transmuted into peace. Anything you accept fully will get you there, will take you into peace. This is the miracle of surrender.

—Eckhart Tolle

JESUS REALIZED THAT every genuine expression of love grows out of a consistent and total surrender to God. In a real sense, faith is total surrender to God.

—MARTIN LUTHER KING, JR.

LIMITLESS, undying love
that shines around me like a million suns
 it calls me on and on, across the universe.
—JOHN LENNON AND PAUL MCCARTNEY

NONVIOLENCE means universal love.
—MOHANDAS GANDHI

Contents

Part Two
Living within the Boundaries
of Nonviolence

Part Three
Becoming a Channel of God's Peace
in a Peaceless World

Preface

When the pandemic hit in 2020, I was living alone in a cabin with a black-and-white cat on a thousand-acre ranch right along the Pacific Ocean just south of Big Sur, California. I had to bring in water and wood for the stove, but otherwise it was magical. I had just published a collection of meditations on the psalms, *Praise Be Peace: Psalms of Peace and Nonviolence in a Time of War and Climate Change*, and was preparing to embark on a thirty-city book tour. I was also organizing a national conference on nonviolence featuring many nationally known speakers and activists, followed by a peace vigil outside the National Nuclear Weapons Laboratories in Los Alamos, New Mexico, on August 6 and 9, 2020, to mark the seventy-fifth anniversary of the US atomic bombing of Hiroshima and Nagasaki.

I was driving into Santa Fe for my second speaking event on March 12 when the pandemic struck. The news broke that actor Tom Hanks had COVID, and suddenly, the whole country realized how serious this was. The next morning, within forty-five minutes, all my speaking events were canceled. I turned around and drove back to Big Sur. I had no idea what lay in store.

Suddenly, I was alone with time on my hands. Thinking this might last just a few months, I decided to try to use the time wisely for more prayer, reflection, and long walks along the coast. I also decided to join the local gym, and for the first time in my life, to take exercise classes.

There were fifteen of us, men and women, all over fifty-five, and a young woman instructor named Heidi. She had us for an hour, three mornings a week. She would have made a good drill sergeant. She pushed us, ordered us, and commanded us to keep moving nonstop till we dropped, and we did. By the end, every one of us was dripping with sweat and exhausted. I often spent the rest of the day recovering, unable to move.

As the lockdown slowly began, I felt moved to write about the Gospels and, over time, threw myself into writing my life's work, *The Gospel of Peace: A Commentary on Matthew, Mark, and Luke from the Perspective of Nonviolence*, a mammoth study of the Synoptic Gospels line by line as if Gandhi and Dr. King were pointing out each instance of Jesus's spectacular nonviolence.

After a few months, Heidi moved on. While most stores were shut down, our gym was still open, so the classes continued. A new instructor showed up. Will was twenty-four, a recent college graduate, a gifted gym teacher, and just as determined to get us old folks into shape. One day we began talking, and he asked, to my surprise, if I would offer him spiritual direction.

I've served as a spiritual director for many people throughout my life. I have also had my own spiritual director since 1980. For me, a spiritual director is someone to meet with once a month or so to discuss the presence of God in one's life, and how God might be trying to guide us. As a spiritual director, I see myself as a coach, someone who asks repeatedly, "Where is God in your life?" and "What is God saying to you?" Then I point out how the person is evading and resisting God, and I urge the person to go back to God, be with God, and do God's will. In other words, a spiritual director is someone who tries to get you in spiritual shape. We all need such coaching.

Not knowing where this would lead, I said yes to Will, and within a few weeks we began to meet for spiritual direction. It turned out that Will had studied in college to be a journalist and liked to write. And so, as our town began to shut down, we began to include writing sessions along with our spiritual conversation at the rare coffee shops that remained open.

Between our conversations, our writing practice, my intense study of nonviolence in the Gospels, and the solitude of lockdown cabin life, I began to realize that Will's invitation to offer spiritual direction was offering something more than I had expected. I began to be drawn to a new understanding of the spiritual life as total surrender to the God of Peace. That's how this book was born. Rather than an instruction manual, these reflections are a sharing of our conversation, meditation, and exploration, in many cases returning to themes I have explored throughout my life, but seen now through a particular lens. If I sound like I know what I'm talking about—be warned! I don't. I'm not an expert at any of this. If anything, I'm an expert at *not* surrendering to the God of Peace, despite all my best efforts and claims and postures. Over these years, and through this writing, I've confronted entirely new levels of ego, self-seeking, and efforts to control that have blocked me from God and robbed me of God's peace. The miracle, however, is that through the practice of ongoing surrender and humility before the God of Peace I am beginning to see a new way forward to experience a deeper peace.

"Make sure you tell people from the start," Will said to me the other day at the Blackhorse Café, "that whatever teachings and lessons you are writing about are what you are working on, not what you have perfected." That's the point, he argued.

Of course, I agreed. If I sound preachy in the pages that follow, that's not just an occupational hazard; I'm preaching to myself first of all. I'm trying to get myself to practice what I believe. The teachings and lessons that follow are *what I struggle with, what I'm working on*, not necessarily what I live and practice, much as I would like to say otherwise. These teachings are my own challenges and hurdles. Hopefully, the reader will hear my own struggle, first and foremost, as much as Will's, to do God's will, and to surrender to the God of Universal Love and Peace.

Many of these lessons have been taught before in classic texts of Catholic spirituality. These include the great work by the French Jesuit Jean-Pierre de Caussade, *Abandonment to Divine Providence*. Born in the late seventeenth century, this spiritual director served a small convent of French nuns and taught them about "the sacrament of the present moment," encouraging them to abandon themselves completely to God in the present moment every day. These teachings can also be found in that classic work *The Practice of the Presence of God* by the seventeenth-century Carmelite friar Brother Lawrence. He taught that every task and encounter of daily life, which in his case largely consisted of working in the kitchen, could become a kind of prayer if performed in conscious awareness of the presence of God.

As I began to experiment with this spiritual practice as a way to live out the nonviolence described by Gandhi and Dr. King, I wondered about the social implications of a life surrendered to the God of Peace in the present moment. In other words, if God is universal love, universal compassion, and universal peace, and if we surrender our wills and our lives on a daily basis to this gentle, loving God, doesn't it follow that over time we will become people of universal love, universal compassion, and universal peace, that is, people of total, Godly nonviolence? In a world of universal violence and war, there are surely political implications and consequences of surrendering to the God of Universal Love and Peace.

That question became my focus. What does abandonment to Divine Providence mean in a world of immense human suffering and violence? As I studied the Gospels throughout those days, it seemed to me that surrendering ourselves to the will of God as the nonviolent Jesus did would lead us on the same path that he took and endured. We would naturally begin nonviolently to resist all that is not the will of God, starting with our own greed, violence, racism, and environmental destruction.

These reflections, which I shared with Will, forced me to grapple with my own failings and weaknesses. In a new search to give myself to God more fully, I prayed that God might use me to do God's will, even in all my brokenness. Instead of feeling depressed at my stubborn, egocentric selfishness, I was excited about the challenge, the invitation, the path, and the direction this resolution offered. I resolved that if I fell down every single day in my effort to do God's will, no matter, I would try to get up again, surrender to God all over again, and go forward. Since then, the adventure of life has only grown deeper and more exciting. I know now that the journey's the thing. We make progress one step at a time. Progress, not perfection, is the goal.

I'm grateful to Will, whose initiative and friendship inspired me to write these reflections. I thank him for his generosity in allowing me to share some of his experience. Let me add that, in order to protect his privacy, I am not using his real name.

I've structured the book like one of Thich Nhat Hanh's many beautiful small books, with short sections on a theme, divided into three general parts: first, on surrendering to God; second, on living out the nonviolence of God in our day to day lives; and third, pursuing the social implications and consequences of doing the will of the God of Universal Love and Peace.

You will notice here, as with Thich Nhat Hanh's books, that the little sections tend to echo one another, returning often to the spiritual practice of surrendering to the God of Peace. Each time this begins to feel repetitive to you, each time you begin to skim or check out when you read some version of this spiritual invitation, I invite you to ask yourself, "What does this mean to me right now?" even if you just asked yourself that same question on the previous page. The point is to keep at it, to keep digging, to keep hearing the message until it sinks in. If it feels repetitive, remember that the teaching is about a repetitive way of living. Each moment of our lives invites us all over again to surrender to the God of Universal Love and Peace. As you may know, meditation rarely feels "new" or "exciting," but if we sit with ourselves and our God, explore whatever blocks us from God, and finally let go, we will go deeper into God, and that is the point, that is the journey, that is the lesson. There, in those deep places, we experience God's mercy all over again in new, fresh ways.

I share these offerings in the hope that they may encourage your own pilgrimage of peace, that you might discover new insights, take new steps forward, surrender yourself anew to the God of Universal Love and Peace, and be sent forth in God's global grassroots movement of nonviolence to spread peace, justice, and love far and wide among all people and all creation.

—JOHN DEAR

Opening Prayer

God of Peace,

Thank you for all the blessings of life, love, and peace that you give us.

Be with me now as I reflect on your gift of peace to me and all humanity.

Help me open my heart and my mind to welcome your gift of peace and do your will of peace.

Touch me, heal me, disarm me, and pour out your Holy Spirit upon me,

That I may be filled with your peace, live in your peace, and walk forward in your peace and love from this day onward.

Take away all that is not of your peace in me that I might be centered in your peace.

Help me to share your peace with all those I meet. Let me be a beacon of your peace.

Give me the grace to surrender myself over
and over again to you so that you live
through me, your peace shines through
me, you make peace through me, and
you spread your peace to others through
me.

Guide me along the journey of universal
love and nonviolence that I may truly
be your beloved child, your holy peacemaker, until I dwell forever with you, the
God of Universal Love and Peace. Amen.

Part One

∽

Surrendering to the God of Peace

ONCE YOU THINK you've got God in your pocket—that you understand the great Mystery—religion always becomes arrogant and idolatrous, where we love our explanation of God more than actually falling in love with God. . . . God refuses to ever be an object of the intellect but is only known by those who enter into love and surrender.

—RICHARD ROHR

PEACE COMES FROM not needing to control everything and not needing to have everything and not needing to surpass everyone and not needing to know everything and not needing to have everyone else be like me.

—JOAN CHITTISTER

THE SPIRITUAL LIFE is not about gaining control but losing control.

—RICHARD ROHR

WHEN WE SUBMIT ourselves fully to God's will, everything will turn out for the good. May things come about as God wants.

—FRANZ JÄGERSTÄTTER

Turning toward Universal Love and Peace

So there I was working out in gym class one day in the summer of 2020, in the early days of the COVID pandemic, and Will, the new, young gym instructor, said to me, "I've been reading about you and your work online, and I would like you to be my guru."

I've been called a lot of things, but never a guru, so I laughed. I agreed to meet with him and talk about the spiritual life. I said I would become his spiritual director.

When we first sat down to talk, I asked him, "Do you believe in God?"

"No," he said.

"Okay," I said. "What do you believe in?"

After thinking about it, he answered, "I believe in truth and love and compassion."

"That works for me," I said.

Christians believe that God is truth, love, and compassion, I said. Gandhi went so far as to say, "Truth is God." The New Testament says, "God is love." My problem, I continued, is with the word *love*. "It's lost its meaning. The New Testament uses the Greek word *agape,* which means unconditional, all-encompassing, nonviolent, universal love. So I think of God as Universal Love."

"That works for me," he said. "I want to learn how to meditate because when I took a class in world religions in college, I saw how important it is for a well-rounded life."

"Okay," I said, "if you want to step into the spiritual life and learn about prayer and meditation, try to spend thirty minutes in silence every day and ask Universal Love to be with you and speak to you. This is what I try to do. In other words, instead of talking about the God of Universal Love or the spiritual life, go and experience Universal Love, then get back to me."

He had never been to church, and had no interest in church, but he was interested in meditation, so he accepted the challenge.

$\backsim$

Becoming an Extension of Universal Love and Peace

A week later Will came over to visit me in my little cabin along the Central Coast. He told me that he had been sitting in silent meditation every day and had been focusing on his breath, so that he was sitting very still and breathing consciously. Then one day he became overwhelmed with a sense of peace and joy that he had never known before. He felt he was in the presence of Universal Love. He'd simply never had an experience like it. He cried while trying to describe it.

I admit that I was surprised that he had achieved such quick rewards from his practice. But over the decades I had heard this before. If we open our hearts and souls to God, God can rush in like a flood and fill us with love and peace.

Already, Will's experience of Universal Love had led him to moments of bliss in which he felt unconditionally loved, and realized that every human being was unconditionally loved and that, from now on, he too could practice unconditional love toward every human being and all creation.

In that profound spiritual moment, he told me, he realized his calling in life: "I'm created to be an extension of Universal Love."

Will set me thinking. I had never heard the phrase before, though I remembered the famous prayer attributed to St. Francis, "Make me an instrument of your peace." Will's announcement led me to ask: How do we become extensions of God's universal love and peace; how do we help each other become extensions of God's universal love?

"That is your mission for the rest of your life," I told him. "You are called to be 'an extension of Universal Love.' I hope you can remember that from now on."

I began to think that not one of us can do this on our own. If we want to know God, serve God, and give ourselves to God to the point that we are transformed into extensions of God's universal love and peace, then we have to do what the God of Universal Love and Peace wants—not what we want, not how we think things should be done, not with any sense of knowing better than God, and certainly not for our own credit. We need the God of Universal Love to do this through us, and in us. All we have to do is give ourselves over to Universal Love, to the God of Universal Love, every moment, for the rest of our lives.

Right there, that sounds impossible. And yet, Jesus says, with God all things are possible. We can do this if we make this our number-one priority, our primary focus, our purpose in life. We turn to God over and over again throughout our day so that we are living a daily journey of spiritual progress and rigorous growth in God, in God's universal love and peace. We lose ourselves in God, in Universal Love, and in the process, find ourselves.

As I thought about this, I realized how little I really understood it, and how much I needed to live this intentionally in my own life.

Becoming an extension of Universal Love and Peace requires that we take time each day in quiet meditation to open our hearts, our minds, and our spirits to the God who is Universal Love and Peace, so that God's qualities fill us, dwell in us, and work through us. Through this daily practice, we begin to live out God's universal love and peace more and more in thought, word and deed.

Over time, as we consciously center ourselves in God's love and peace, we see things differently and live differently. We feel empathy and compassion for every human being and for all of creation. God's nonviolence and compassion become more deeply rooted in us and we find new hope and energy to keep going forward in Universal Love toward everyone and all creation. We eagerly embark each day in the adventure of Universal Love, which means we begin to side with the poor, the oppressed, the marginalized, the enemy, and all those targeted by hate and war. We bring Universal Love to our sisters and brothers in need at home and abroad. We let our love widen to embrace all creatures and Mother Earth in compassion and total nonviolence.

All of this goes against the way of the world. So we return to meditation, reflect on our progress, and receive strength to start anew each day so that over time, the way of Universal Love and Peace becomes our new normal, our ordinary way of life. For this, we were created. We have found our purpose! Life is good!

Anyone can sit in silence with our God, with Universal Love, at any moment and reconnect and live in that relationship, I told Will. No matter where we are, or what is happening, we can take a breath, center ourselves in our quiet breathing, enter the presence of God, of Universal Love, and fulfill our true calling. If we open ourselves to Universal Love, Universal Love will come and be with us. We will experience a peace and a joy we have never known. If we open our hearts and lives to this Spirit of Universal Love, then we will be given peace. Everything else will fall away because God, Universal Love, has been invited to be fully present to us.

ॐ

The Practice of Meditation

Not long after our conversation on Universal Love, Will came back doubting the whole experience. When he sat in meditation, he said, he did not always feel the presence and bliss of Universal Love and Peace.

"When I go to sit in meditation," he said, "my mind starts racing. I think all kinds of thoughts about life, work, and girls, and I can't center myself. I'm just fooling myself."

This was hardly surprising, I told him. That's the way the mind works. Maybe for the first time in your life you're noticing your mind. It's like a TV with five hundred channels and endless crazy shows. Your mind keeps changing channels and letting these thoughts and images rule your life. That's what every human being does. The trick is to learn how to control the TV in your mind, to not change channels mindlessly but to stay centered on the channel of the highest good, the greatest peace, the widest love for yourself and humanity—intentionally, mindfully, regularly. The invitation of the spiritual life is to sit down, become quiet, relax, notice your breathing in and out, notice your thoughts and your breath, let the mind settle, open your heart, and try to be mindful and centered on one channel—on God, God's channel of Universal Love and Peace.

You will never be able to do this perfectly, I told Will. It will be like this till the day you die, but you can slow down the never-ending newsreel of the mind and experience profound moments of stillness and true peace. Over time, the love of God, the fullness of Universal Love, becomes a deep-down contentment, as if you were resting in the arms of Universal Love.

Drawing on an example from Thich Nhat Hanh, I said it's like a glass of fresh apple juice. If you pour the juice into the glass and stir it, it clouds up with brown pulp. But if you let it sit and settle down, even for hours, it clears up. Your mind is like that. As you learn to enjoy sitting in peace and noticing your breath, and opening yourself to God's universal love and peace, your mind calms down and you feel more at peace. If you find yourself distracted and thinking, you can whisper to yourself, "That's just a thought," and return to your breath, to Universal Love. Over time, it becomes easier and you learn to live your daily life out of these deep inner moments of connection with Universal Love. You prefer them to the endless, mindless wanderings of your mind. As you grow in awareness of your unconscious mindlessness, you seek ways to cultivate mindfulness.

The Buddhists emphasize the importance of gently noticing your breath—breathing in and breathing out—as an antidote to your racing mind and general peacelessness. As you notice yourself breathing in and out naturally, your mind settles down, peace comes upon you, and you are available should Universal Love decide to show up. "Try it, you'll see," I suggested to Will.

Check-in Time with the God of Universal Love and Peace

The path of peace starts with quiet meditation, I kept insisting to Will. When I speak of the path of peace, I refer to a daily practice that helps us deal with frustration, struggle, hard emotions, and the world itself, indeed, everything that is not peaceful. This is not a burden, not a problem, not an obligation, and not a privilege. It is a basic human exercise necessary for our ongoing spiritual growth, and for life itself. Without it, we flail about in confusion, foolishness, illusion, and violence. With meditation, we regain our focus, our purpose, and our inner strength all over again each day. We return to our innate peace and nonviolence and reclaim our humanity. More, we return to the God of Peace and are empowered to step into the world of war as people of peace.

This is not brain surgery, I suggested to Will. All we have to do is take thirty minutes or so every day to sit by ourselves in silence and enter the presence of God, of Universal Love. There we can breathe, let our minds focus on our breath, and dwell in that presence. We can talk intimately to God, listen for God, sit with God, and rest in God. In peace, we learn how to adore the God of Peace. In love, we feel ourselves embraced by Universal Love. This becomes the center of our day, the highlight of our ordinary life. Just consider this: we get to be with the Holy, with the very Source of all love and peace!

Each time I tried to says these things to Will, I began to get carried away with my own excitement, but he was a good sport about my enthusiasm.

Along the way, over time, I suggested, we need to let go of violence. We gently begin to "non-cooperate" with the world's violence, as Gandhi put it. Slowly over time, we grow out of our kindergarten-level spirituality and theology and mature into Universal Love and Peace. We let go of false images of God—a punitive, vindictive, punishing deity who is eager to throw us all into the fires of hell. Instead, to our surprise, we meet the Spirit of the living God, who loves us unconditionally, who is actually interested in us, who likes us and likes being with us. We move beyond our childish, puny false god and into the mystery of God as Universal Love, Universal Compassion, and Universal Peace.

Daily meditation can open the space where we become conscious of our intimate relationship with God throughout the rest of the day. This becomes our daily, formal check-in time with God. We give God, Universal Love, our full, undivided attention. Over time, this daily practice heals us, disarms us, and leads us into a gentler, more nonviolent life, one that can love, serve, disarm, and heal others. Eventually, we find we cannot live without our daily meditation, without this inner search for the presence of the God who loves us. Meditation becomes essential to our survival in this peaceless world. It's like oxygen to a drowning man.

If we persist in this practice, over time we find ourselves more and more living every moment in God, in Universal Love. As we do that, life gets better. This has been my experience, I confessed to Will. I'm not perfect by any means—far from it!—but I've found that the more I center myself on God, on Universal Love, the better life is, the happier I am, and the more useful I become.

∽

The Difference Meditation Makes

Will was smiling the next time we met. "Whenever I meditate in the morning, my whole day feels better," he said. "When I don't meditate, I'm not myself. If something goes wrong or someone says something hurtful, I'm ready to snap back. But when I meditate, I'm more present, more centered and a little more thoughtful, less ready to snap at someone, and more present and compassionate toward others."

I responded that this is how the spiritual life works, how we live the way of peace. This is what it feels like to become an extension of Universal Love, to live and breathe in God's peace. If we center ourselves every day during our quiet meditation, we will begin to live in God's spirit of peace and universal love, and we will notice the difference. We become less selfish, egocentric, mean, and violent. We start to feel and radiate God's spirit. We literally feel better, and discover that we enjoy spending time with God every day and sharing that love and peace with others.

Without this basis in the Universal Love and Peace of God, we remain stuck in the rut of mindlessness, letting our egos and selfishness run our lives, hurting others, and eventually carrying on the world's spirit of violence and hate. The culture of violence around us does not encourage us to dwell in peace and express love toward one another. That's considered weakness, even though, in fact, it's true strength. But if we begin to root our daily life in the practice of dwelling with God, then we will notice a concrete difference in how we feel. Over time, we will become more peaceful and loving. This becomes our natural way of being in the world.

I was quick to add that no one can make another person do this. Each of us has to choose to spend this time and attention in God's presence. It will not come to you otherwise. Using an example I knew he would appreciate, I said it's like exercise, getting into shape, and losing weight. You have to make it a priority of your life. You have to want it. You have to make room for it. You have to carve out quality time in your schedule for it. You want to be with God, feel God's love and peace, and share those gifts for the rest of your life. You don't want to waste any more time in the world's insane peacelessness.

After this pep talk, Will looked at me as if I were crazy, but he agreed to give it a try.

❧

Living in Relationship with the God of Peace and Universal Love

In our first conversation Will had told me he didn't believe in God. That is how we entered into our talk about Universal Love. But I quickly found myself speaking of God, because that is what came naturally to me. I asked his forgiveness if instead of Universal Love I sometimes spoke of God. He didn't object. But I encouraged him to imagine entering into a relationship with a Living Source that is beneath all things and holds the universe together.

Imagine, I said, that this Personal Being of Infinite Love wants to be your friend, to be with you, to spend time with you, to give you every blessing of peace and love. What's not to like? Who doesn't want to sit with someone who loves us unconditionally? Why don't we all want this?

That's how we make the transition from approaching meditation as a duty to something we can't wait to do. The key here is that you are entering an intimate *relationship* with God, I told my friend. Once you understand that you are in a relationship with God and are invited deeper into intimacy with God, then you will enjoy meditation. It becomes the one place where you are truly safe and secure. There, you can be free and whole as you truly are. You can tell God all your secrets and problems, ask for God's help and guidance, thank God for all the blessings, and feel renewed and empowered to go forward with new energy in God's spirit. This has been my experience in the best and the worst of times.

Gradually, we will learn not to seek feelings of bliss but to enjoy just sitting with God. Over time, any negative childhood images of a false, punishing, violent god fade away. We become accustomed to dwelling together in peaceful silence with our loving God, like two old friends sitting quietly on a park bench holding hands. Through this intimacy with God, we glimpse a peace not of this world, and that glimpse, that relationship, that intimacy, becomes our life.

ೲ

The Secret of Life:
Surrendering to the God of Peace

It has taken me a lifetime to learn the secret of the spiritual life. I tried to say this to Will with honesty and without self-righteousness. God is universally loving and infinitely peaceful! That means, as Jesus teaches—and later, Gandhi, Dr. King, and Dorothy Day—that God, by nature, is totally nonviolent. That means that God never coerces us but gives each of us complete free will. God allows us to make our own choices, and it is not consistent with God's love to force us to love God or make one choice over another.

The problem is that in our freedom, we have grown used to being in control and doing what we want. Our lives are ruled by self-will, which is limited and selfish. Our will serves only our ego, pride, and honor. It wants comfort, pleasure, riches, and power, even though none of these things bring lasting peace or happiness or serve the God of Universal Love. The more we want for ourselves, the more we struggle to gain what we want and what we can't have, the more pain and suffering we generate for ourselves and others.

Self-will always obsesses over itself and cannot give any room to others and certainly not to God. In following the will's inclinations, we forget God's loving kindness and gentleness toward us. We deliberately, consciously turn away from God and, in doing so, sever our ties to real love and peace. As problems, difficulties, and crises arise, we blame God and resent God for not being there for us, even though we ourselves long ago rejected God. And we resent anyone who invites us to a more Godly, spiritual, peace-filled, loving, nonviolent life. With every downhill step, we fall deeper into the darkness of our selfishness and inner violence. As self-will leads us to reject the loving and wise will of God, we descend further into peacelessness, violence, and death.

The secret to the path of peace, then, is to renounce our self-will and surrender our will entirely to the God of Peace and Universal Love. We must do this every day, every moment from now on. If we want to be extensions of Universal Love, we must surrender our will over and over to Universal Love, so that we are transformed without any effort on our part into extensions of Universal Love.

Some people fight God their whole life, never knowing peace, and never surrendering until their last breath. They live in misery because they are never satisfied, never peaceful, never present, always trying to be in control. Along the way, they hurt everyone in their path and unconsciously leave a trail of wreckage behind them. Everyone around them becomes a victim of their peacelessness. We all do this to varying degrees. But now we are learning to surrender ourselves to the God of Peace, and to let God's peace flow through us freely.

Our ongoing surrender creates a place in which God can heal our relationships and resolve our problems. More than that, God will use us to help others as God helped us. This was always God's plan—to use us, if we are willing, to draw us into God's universal love and peace and, in the process, spread God's love and peace far and wide through us as God sees best.

Sooner or later, whether it's today or our last day, we will discover the freedom and peace of total surrender to God, and we'll wish we had come to that place long before. The sooner we surrender everything to God, the better everything will be.

❧

Our New Mantra

As we begin the daily practice of surrender to the God of Peace, we discover that this practice is at once harder and easier than we imagined. It's as simple as taking the next breath, yet it exposes a stubborn hard-heartedness and our desire to be in control. That's when we realize that our surrendering is not just a daily practice, but a minute-by-minute practice.

We see this in the life of the peacemaking Jesus, who was totally devoted to the God of Peace he called his beloved Father, or Abba (which could be translated as "Daddy"). I think he surrendered every moment of his life to God, over and over again. In doing so, he could walk into the world and proclaim God's reign of universal love, peace, and nonviolence. He could show us what living in God looks like through his universal love and compassion and acts of public peacemaking, even in his march to Jerusalem, where he confronted imperial injustice and the religious and imperial authorities who subsequently executed him.

In the Garden of Gethsemane, just before he was arrested, the Gospels report that he prayed one single prayer, "Not my will, but your will be done." That prayer is embedded in the prayer he earlier taught his disciples, now known as The Lord's Prayer: "Your kingdom come; Your will be done, on earth as it is in heaven."

Jesus could endure torture and execution because he remained in a state of complete surrender to God. He maintained his nonviolence and forgave his murderers. His last whispered words were a stunning, consistent surrender to God: "Father, forgive them, they know not what they do. Into your hands, I commend my spirit."

Notice that he is not debating "my will" vs. "God's will." Jesus's goal, and the goal for all of us, is to be able to live out this statement every day: "God's will *is* my will." That's why Jesus will speak in John's Gospel about doing nothing on his own but only what he sees God doing and what God tells him to do. Jesus is never in control of his life. He has surrendered himself completely to God every day, every hour, every moment, so that he embodies peace and love, even as all hell is breaking loose around him. From him we can learn that we can do nothing on our own, but if we surrender ourselves to God, God can support us and work miracles through us.

Recently, while walking on the beautiful grounds of the monastery in Big Sur, I told my spiritual director that I think this might be the ultimate prayer, the one prayer every human being ought to repeat throughout their day: "Not my will, but your will be done." I suggested that it should become our new mantra. My monk friend turned to me and said quietly, "I say that prayer a thousand times a day." I was stunned, and I believed him. I thought I was making progress saying it twenty times a day, and on bad days, one hundred times. But way more is required. This is the prayer we should say under our breath at all times, so that the focus from now on is not ourselves but the living God.

✍

The Surrendered Life

Will had moved away to work as the sports manager and gym instructor at a resort in another country. We talked on the phone occasionally about our work and the daily practice of surrender. One day I texted him, "The more you surrender to God, the less you have to struggle."

"That's a game-changer," he texted back.

"Everything becomes easier because it is now in God's hands," I later told him. "It's out of your control, so why worry?" (As usual, I was really speaking to myself. He was helping me more than I was helping him.) You don't have to worry; you don't have to be afraid; you don't have to be anxious; you don't have to be desperate, insecure, doubtful, confused, ashamed, self-centered, selfish, mean, or violent in any way. A truly surrendered person can let go of all that. Everything is being taken care of in the great Spirit of Universal Love and Peace. As my teacher Daniel Berrigan told me long ago, "Our lives are in better hands than our own."

God knows way better than we do what is best for us, so we can trust God and trust that as we surrender more and more every day, throughout our day, all will be well. In fact, things do get better. We can relax, do the work that's been given us to do, serve and love the people around us, contribute to the world's peace and disarmament, and enjoy the present moment of God's peace among creation.

When we surrender to the God of Peace, we no longer need to go down the rabbit hole. Someone else lifts us up, holds us by the hand, guides us, leads us, and protects us. We are taken care of, we are loved, even comforted, like a little child.

Will seemed encouraged by all this and, as he started to practice it, he began to trust more and more in Universal Love, in God. So did I.

౭౨

Archbishop Tutu and God's Gift of Free Will

As we met over the years at local coffee shops or sometimes in my cabin where the walls were covered with photos of my heroes and saints, I told Will about some of my teachers, the many peacemakers I have known and loved. One day I shared the story of my visit with Archbishop Desmond Tutu in Cape Town, South Africa.

"I'm so glad I'm not God," Tutu said to me as we drank coffee and ate lunch in the corner of his office.

What? I remembered thinking to myself as he talked. I had no idea why he was saying this or the wisdom he was trying to impart to me.

I had gone to South Africa on a one-month pilgrimage with friends to see Johannesburg and Soweto, visit the Gandhi sites in Durban and Pietermaritzberg, pray at the home of Steve Biko and the prison on Robben Island, and meet those who resisted apartheid and continued the struggle to build a rainbow nation. But my visit with

Archbishop Tutu at the end of the journey was the high-light. I had corresponded with him for many years over the internet (he called me his "pen pal"), and I knew he was not well and growing older and frailer. But I found him to be as feisty as ever.

He was my guru, my spiritual director, teacher, and friend.

"Think of the patience of God, waiting for us to get it, waiting for us to organize movements for justice and peace," he said to me. "So few people see that we're all sisters and brothers!" he continued. "Imagine what God went through during the Holocaust," he said looking off to the side, "waiting while some of his children killed his other children and there was nothing he could do. God is omnipotent and omnipresent but he has decided to gift us with the gift of freedom, to let us choose to accept goodness and love or not, and because God gave us this gift of freedom, this gift of free will, God cannot intervene. So this omnipotent God is completely weak and powerless before the evil we do. This is the God we have. God is very weak. I am so glad I am not God and that God is God."

I was astonished. I had not expected him to launch into such a profound reflection about the mystery of God and free will. Nor had I expected him to start weeping as he talked about the helplessness of our loving God as we continue to wage war and destroy the planet. Nor did I understand any of it.

But I shouldn't have been surprised. Archbishop Tutu was one of the greatest prophets in history. His journey is mythic—from serving the churches throughout Africa during the 1970s and 1980s to his leadership in the World Council of Churches and the South African Council of Churches, and as bishop and archbishop; to his public stand against the evil apartheid system; his speeches to millions, his endless call for justice; to the massive anti-apartheid funerals he officiated, the marches and prayer vigils he led, his visits to prisoners and their families, his civil disobedience; to the times he intervened and saved those about to be killed; to the many attacks and death threats he faced; to his steadfast adherence to nonviolence; to his ground-breaking work with the Truth and Reconciliation Commission; to his global advocacy for justice with countless causes, individuals and organizations; and, finally, to his exemplary leadership, faith, and hope. Throughout all of this he remained grounded in daily prayer, underlying fidelity, and radiant peace and joy.

I remember hearing him speak at the National Cathedral in Washington, DC, sometime around 1986. It was at the height of the struggle against apartheid, and the world was waking up to its horrors. He had just come from Soweto, where an elderly woman told him that she woke every morning at 2:00 a.m. and spent one hour solemnly begging God for an end to apartheid.

"I know we will win now," he said through tears, "because God cannot resist the prayer of that poor old woman."

"We do not have the right to give up this work," he told me as he wept that day in Cape Town. "Our sisters and brothers are suffering around the world, so we have to keep working for peace and justice till we die." Then, to my amazement, he announced that he was flying to Iran the next morning to call for peace. He was relentless, despite his own poor health and the demands made upon him.

"How do you keep going?" I asked.

"My favorite prophet is Jeremiah," he answered. "Do you know why? Because he cries a lot!" Then he leaned close to me and whispered, "I cry a lot, too. I cry every day. But think how much God cries! We have a God who weeps. God weeps because we don't get it, because we don't understand that we are all sisters and brothers. So I cry a lot and always have. But I also laugh a lot, too." With that he let out an uproarious laugh and started teasing me for having what he described as a baby face, leaving my friends in stitches as he took delight in this playful banter. What great fun he was!

"Never give up, John," he said as I was leaving, his arm around me. "Never give up! You and I have to work for peace and justice until the day we die!"

Desmond Tutu exemplified for me a life surrendered to the God of Universal Love and Peace, I told Will. He showed us what that life looks like. His life was not his own; it belonged entirely to God, and so he was always at the service of humanity, creation, justice, and peace, as well as his family and all those he encountered along the way. Because he was surrendered to God, he became an extension—you might say an incarnation or embodiment—of universal love and peace. He learned to move far beyond anger, fear, and despair to grieve the world's insane violence, to take public nonviolent action to stop it, but also to enjoy the fullness of life as well.

We can all live that level of committed, honest peacemaking if we surrender ourselves to the God of Peace over and over again as he did.

Humility Is the Way

Once during another visit at the coffee shop I said to Will, "The shocking revelation of this practice of total surrender to God is not just how it exposes my ego and self-will, but how it opens a doorway I hadn't seen before. It liberates me from my drive to take charge of everything, to be in control." This doorway is the invitation into a space of humility in which not I, but God, is the center of the universe. In this place of humility, God leads and I get to enjoy the ride and watch the miracle unfold.

Even there, over coffee at the Blackhorse Café, on a mild Tuesday afternoon, whispering about humility and God, I felt free in the present moment, in the ordinariness of life, and the beauty of living in God's peace.

And yet I knew, even as I spoke to Will, how far I was from realizing this goal. I always joked with my friends that we each have different spiritual gifts, and I didn't get the gift of humility. But the issue was deeper and more problematic than that. I had been spiritually stuck all my life thinking that I was in charge, that I was greater than most people, and that I knew better than pretty much everyone else. My ego was blinding, out of control, and offensive, but I couldn't see it (even as my relatives and friends did); and when I did see it, I didn't know how to change it. It prevented me from truly surrendering to God.

I think that anything that leads us to humility, compassion, and love is a blessing from God. In the process of letting go into God, I begin to see that my ego, selfishness, and narcissism are great burdens that I no longer need to carry. I don't *need* to be perfect. I don't *need* to control anything or anyone. I don't *need* to play God. In fact, I finally realize that I don't want to be God.

Instead, I could surrender to God all my flaws, imperfections, bad habits, ego, pride, and self-centeredness, indeed my entire being, and God could heal me, give me God's peace, and maybe even use me for God's plan of peace for humanity. That has become my goal—to do what God wants, not what I want, no matter how noble the goal. God's plan, God's will, God's vision is infinitely better than mine.

It has been a long, slow process unfolding over the past sixty-five years. This growing self-realization over the course of a lifetime drove me to my knees. "Beloved God, have mercy on me," I learned to pray. "Jesus, have mercy on me, a sinner." The ancient Jesus Prayer took on new meaning. I began to say: "I surrender everything to you: all my plans, desires, hopes, and ambitions, all my self-will, ego, narcissism, and pride. I let it all go. You do with me what you will. Your will, not mine, be done."

In that way, I have started to experience the freedom and peace of true humility. What a relief! I no longer have to be in charge! I realize that the more I let go of control, the happier, more compassionate, and more peaceful I am. Now, as I write this at age sixty-five, I am finally beginning to understand it, consciously choose it, and live it.

As I shared all this with Will, I studied the expression on his face. "I'm finally learning to surrender to God," I said. "And when I do this, even for my own basic survival, lo and behold, I discover that problems get resolved, everything becomes easier, and I can live and breathe in the peace of the present moment. I can surrender any disturbance, feeling, disorder, crisis, and problem that very moment to God and trust that God will take care of it.

"Through humility, you can become a real extension of Universal Love and do your part publicly to extend that love to others," I suggested. "It is no longer you who lives and breathes, but Universal Love who lives and breathes and works through you. In other words, after a lifetime of mistakes and regrets, this is where I am now, this is what I find most helpful, this is what I want to pass on to you."

⤬

To Hell with Spiritual Pride

Humility before God may be the greatest virtue. Only with true humility before the God of Peace and Love can we know those qualities and extend them to others. We will always have the tendency to take back control and withdraw from God's generosity and wisdom. This leads to all sorts of trouble, and suffering, and even violence and death.

So the question becomes: Do we want to live egocentric or God-centric lives? Can we become God-conscious, God-centered, and God-centric 24/7? That is one way of explaining the journey of life. The God of Peace has given us the freedom to choose to live according to our own egocentric, self-centered will, or God's will of unconditional, universal love and peace. If we keep surrendering our wills to God and try to live only according to God's will, that egocentric will in us has to die so that the Holy Spirit of God can move freely in and through us.

But let's say we do try to surrender to God, to live for the God of Peace and Love every day, to be channels of God's peace and love, to let God run our lives, to experiment more and more with God's will and not our own will. The first thing we will notice is that we will feel better! We will feel more consoled, more peaceful, and more relaxed. Sure, all the problems within us will come up, and we will panic and try to take control of them, but then we will remember that we have surrendered ourselves to God and give them to God and know that they are in better hands than ours. Then, we can let go of anxiety, worry, fear, and self-obsession.

Let's say we keep doing this intentionally day after day, year after year, and we start feeling more peaceful as our lives and relationships, and work improves, and we become positive, helpful people. But now we might become proud of our progress! We are tempted to take all the credit for our growth and to forget that we must rely on God for not only every bit of progress but also every breath we take.

The definition of spiritual pride is thinking that we, not God, are the source of our goodness, of all the good that is happening in us. We want people to know how good and holy we are, how special and wonderful we are. That was the problem with the religious authorities in the Gospels who acted in God's name as if they were in charge, and then started acting as if they were God, and then began judging everyone left and right until, in the end, they helped kill anyone who challenged their authority, including Jesus.

I told Will that only recently had I uncovered a deep-down sense of superiority I had felt toward others my whole life. I think this was a kind of spiritual, emotional sickness, a selfish way I had found to cope early on with the pain of life. That longstanding ego foundation had not only made my life more painful and difficult for me and others, but it had blocked my unhindered access to God. I get in God's way, and I don't even know it. What I'm finding is that the more I try to surrender to God and do God's will, the more I realize how rarely I have actually done so, how deep my self-will runs, and how total my surrender to God must be.

"Feeling superior to others *is* the problem," Will said. He reminded me of Thich Nhat Hanh's call for empathy, that is, that we realize that we all are stuck and doing the best we can, how we are all stuck and called to help one another out of our ruts. My friend Greg Boyle put it this way: he has found that the best way for him to get beyond "us/them" or "I/me/mine" into "nondualism" is to remember that we are all sick, all broken, all in need of healing, all in need of God.

Pride is a dangerous temptation for all those who pursue God and try to live the spiritual life. But there are tools to help us back on the path of humility. As we grow in awareness of our pride and our tendency to dominate, we keep choosing God's will and not our own. We spend more time with God, asking God to take all that away and put us back on track. We learn to give thanks to God morning, noon, and night for everything, and we meditate on all that God has done for us every day of our lives. Then we start to give God all the credit for everything, for anything good we have done, because we know that in the end, we did not do it. God has done all this through us, for us, and in us. We rejoice in what God is doing, and we enjoy watching God resolve our problems and guide our lives.

We need God. We take the teachings of Jesus and the saints to heart and surrender ourselves completely to God time and time again. We go forth in God's peace and love, and give all the credit to God every step of the way. In the process we are slowly freed from the bondage of our self-centeredness, and we can offer real service to others.

✍

From Control Freak
to the Peace of Letting Go

A key part of this journey of surrender to the God of Peace is letting go of control. "Take me," I confessed to Will, "I'm a natural-born control freak. I've tried every form of control, so take my word for it and go in the opposite direction." I could look back on my life and see how I've tried to control everything about my life and everyone everywhere. But I learned one big lesson across a lifetime of primary research: it doesn't work! Not only that, it's an illusion. We are not in control of anything and never were. We could be hit by a truck tomorrow or get cancer or have a heart attack or a stroke. We could be dead in a flash, and then we will suddenly realize how futile were our efforts to control ourselves and others. Then we will see how we wasted our precious lives by trying to stay in control and resisting the wisdom of letting God take care of us and guide us into God's love.

The invitation to surrender all control of ourselves and every aspect of our lives to God is an invitation to freedom. Much to our relief, we will discover that the God of Peace is better at running our lives than we are, that we don't have to be arrogant, self-righteous or in charge, that God is well equipped to handle every moment if we only let God. God can take care of all our faults, defects, brokenness, and wounds. God can sweep away all our hurts, resentments, grudges, anger, bitterness, and hatred. God can sit in our inner driver's seat, and when that happens we can enjoy the ride and feel more peaceful because God is with us. If we let God lead us, God will. If we surrender to God every day and try to do only God's will every day and let God run our lives, we will know a peace not of this world; our lives will be useful and helpful; and we will be much happier.

God is always with us, but our out-of-control efforts to control everything block the full grace of God to lead us.

It's so strange to give up control and consciously let God handle our lives only to receive many new and unexpected graces. Growing in conscious dependence on the God of Universal Love and Peace is the fundamental bottom line of spiritual maturity. We are not the end of life—God is!—and so we want to get moving now on the journey into the fullness of God. The more we experiment with this truth of reality, the more we will want to be led by God and share God's peace with all our sisters and brothers.

It's worth a try, I told my young friend. In this way, God's peace becomes our new normal. We begin to know consciously that God is walking with us, leading us, and guiding us, and we are safe and sound in the God of Peace. More, our lives can truly be of use to one another, even to all of humanity and creation, because we are becoming extensions of God's universal love and peace.

As I told Will, if we want to be extensions of Universal Love, we have to rely on Universal Love 24/7. Think of it this way, I kept telling him: When we trust God and rely on God, that trust opens a valve within us and Universal Love flows through us and out into the world. That, I declared, was my theory, the wisdom I had gained over the course of a lifetime. This was the path I intended to walk from now on, I said. I hoped he would try it too.

∽

Note to Self: Forget Your Self!

The path toward deeper peace requires letting go of self-will and surrendering to God's will consistently, day by day. I'm not talking about putting ourselves down, hurting ourselves, giving in to shame or self-hatred, or being unkind to ourselves. Quite the opposite! When we give up control of ourselves and others, when we surrender ourselves completely to God's love, we learn how to be more loving and peaceful toward ourselves. For some of us, this is the first time we have ever consciously begun to be kind, gentle, or peaceful toward ourselves.

Spiritual teachers have been advising this practice for centuries. They call us to let go of ourselves, forget ourselves, even die to ourselves. To forget one's self in this holy, peaceful practice means taking a good, long, honest, nonjudgmental, compassionate look at ourselves, our habits, and the way we live—particularly our selfishness, egotism, and narcissism. If everything is about us, then we'll never know God or experience God's peace, much less seek God. If we do not surrender ourselves to God, the Source of all that is good and loving and peaceful, then we will be full of ourselves: boring know-it-alls who care only about ourselves.

To forget one's self is to remember God. It means asking each day: How can I serve the God of Peace today? How can I be an extension of God's universal love today? How can I serve others and help relieve someone's suffering today? How can I use the time I have left on earth serving God, disarming others, protecting creation, and welcoming God's reign of peace with justice? Once we make these outwardly focused, other-centered, God-centered questions part of our daily reflection, we begin to step out of ourselves and into the world, doing our part to bring healing, disarmament, reconciliation, justice, and peace. Then, we discover, as the Beatitudes teach, who we already are: the beloved sons and daughters of the God of Peace.

This teaching is at the heart of Sufi mysticism: *When the self is forgotten, then God is remembered.* The Gospels use tougher language. Instead of letting go or forgetting the self, they speak of denying ourselves, even dying to ourselves. If we truly surrender to God, then much within us has to die. All the selfish obsession, idolatry, and violence at the root of our peacelessness has to die so that God's life force of peace and generosity can motivate and empower all that we do. We will no longer be run by the "false self," as Thomas Merton put it, but begin to live in our "true self," in the peace of God, learning to see ourselves as God sees us. We could go further and say that our selfish self is dying and falling away, and now our humble "Spirit self," our true self, our true spirit, our humble being rooted in God, can live freely. This is what Jesus meant when he taught that we have to become like children if we want to enter God's reign of peace. The more we give ourselves to God, the more we become our best selves. This is how we are made.

This was the passionate message I tried to share with Will. Problem was, I struggled to live it as well.

~❧~

The Gratitude List

Gratitude to the God of Peace becomes our pleasant daily practice as we journey out of our egocentric mind into a new God-centric life. Instead of focusing on ourselves and our self-will, we focus on all the gifts that God lavishes upon us. The more we give thanks, the more we recognize that God is behind everything, and so the more we surrender to God and enter God's deep peace and love all over again. Every moment, every breath, every day becomes an occasion for thanksgiving and praise.

Ingratitude is a sign that we are still stuck in our self-will. But as we let go more and more and rely on God's love and wisdom, we discover that we don't need to worry and stress. And when we let go of worry and stress, we're freer to see the gifts we're given, and so our gratitude increases. God is taking care of us 24/7, and life becomes a full-time blessing full of peace and wonder, even as we go through the ordinary struggles of life such as loss, illness, or death.

Whereas before we may have been stuck in our peace-less, egocentric selves, now gratitude becomes our new normal. We make a point to take time throughout our day to give thanks to God for everything. Just as surrender to God becomes a daily, even hourly practice, so does gratitude. Like surrender, gratitude is an action we take. We do not wait to have feelings of gratitude. We practice gratitude; that is, we literally count our blessings, note those blessings, maybe even write down our blessings daily. We say aloud what we are grateful for on a regular, daily basis. We get specific. We thank God for the little things as well as the big things.

Gratitude is one of the first fruits of the surrendered, nonviolent life. It is a sure sign that we are living more and more in God's presence and growing in conscious awareness of God and total dependence on God. If we make gratitude a regular practice throughout our day, we will be transformed and healed into people of authentic peace who radiate the God of Peace.

Some people keep a gratitude list. They write down the things they are grateful for at the end of their day and then thank God for each of them. Others try to name one hundred things they are grateful for as they fall asleep. In this way gratitude becomes a new habit. Gratitude becomes our basic disposition so that we become people who are truly grateful to God and everyone, grateful to be alive!

The gratitude list might seem like a childish exercise, but it holds tremendous spiritual power and wisdom. We can name almost anything, and maybe even everything, because we can always find God's blessing in everything, even in suffering. So, we pray:

> Thank you, God, for my eyesight, my hearing, my heart, my legs, my hands, my voice, my mind, my soul.
>
> Thank you for this moment, this day, my life, my breath.
>
> Thank you for all my friends and family, for everyone I have ever met, for every creature, for the wonders of creation.
>
> Thank you for that bluebird, that hawk, that squirrel, these old trees, these leaves, this running creek.
>
> Thank you for the sun and the moon, the stars and the sky, the hills and the mountains, the beaches, and the oceans.
>
> Thank you for the possibilities of peace, hope, life, and love, for every instance of mercy, compassion, and kindness.
>
> Thank you for the great saints and peacemakers of history, and all the ones I have known personally.

Thank you for you, God of Peace, for every blessing of peace you give me and for calling me to new life and the depths of peace in you.

Thank you for everyone around the world who is speaking out and taking public action for universal love, justice, disarmament, and global nonviolent conflict resolution.

Thank you for doing all these things and for inviting us to live here and now in your reign of peace on earth.

Thank you for taking care of me and all of us.

Thank you for giving us your gracious gift of free will, for letting us choose to do your will instead of our own selfish will. Thank you for being so good, so gentle, so loving, so peaceful.

Thank you.

Prayer

God of Peace,
I Surrender Everything to You

God of Peace,

Thank you for all the blessings of life, love,
and peace that you give me.

Thank you for healing me, disarming me,
and guiding me on your path of peace
and love.

Help me to do your will of peace and love
always, to live *in* you, *for* you, and *with*
you.

I cannot do this on my own, so I surrender
myself to you, God of Peace.

Let me do your will, not my will, from
now on.

You will that I live in your peace, love,
compassion, and nonviolence every
moment of every day, that I be a channel of your peace, love, compassion, and
nonviolence.

Give me the grace to be surrendered to
you, to live a surrendered life, that I
might live and breathe in your peace and
love.

Take away everything within me that is not
of your peace and love, that I may truly
serve you and others, and spread your
peace and love among everyone I meet
and as far as I can reach.

Thank you for being my strength, my rock,
my gentle, loving God. May you guide
me, lead me, live in me now and always.
Amen.

Part Two

❧

Living within the Boundaries of Nonviolence

NEVER BE IN a hurry; do everything quietly and in a calm spirit. Do not lose your inner peace for anything whatsoever, even if your whole world seems upset.

—St. Francis de Sales

IF YOU ARE depressed you are living in the past; if you are anxious you are living in the future; if you are at peace, you are living in the present.

—Lao Tzu

THOSE WHO ARE attracted to nonviolence should, according to their ability and opportunity, join the experiment.

—Mohandas Gandhi

How Do I Keep from Getting Mad and Snapping at Someone?

Will met me at the Blackhorse Café and announced that he had noticed a major difference in his mood on the days he meditated compared to the days he did not meditate. When he meditated in the morning, it changed the tone of his whole day. He felt better about himself and was happy to be around others and help people during his work. On days he did not meditate, he felt restless, agitated, and more on edge. He was not centered or his best self. His guard was down, and at the slightest provocation he might snap at someone, whether he wanted to or not.

The other day someone at his workplace had voiced a slight put down of him, and he immediately wanted to blow up at the person. He was raging inside, made a sharp comment in response, and walked away. Later he regretted his reaction and felt bad. "What should I have done?" he asked me. "How do I keep from getting mad and snapping at someone, even if someone puts me down?"

"Did you meditate that morning?" I asked. "Did you begin your day centered in the God of Universal Love, with the intention of becoming an extension of Universal Love?"

"No," he answered. "I forgot to meditate."

I reminded him that if you meditate every day, you remember Universal Love and your rock-bottom desire to be an extension of Universal Love. Or, at least, since you are a bit more grounded in Universal Love, you have some awareness of other, more nonviolent ways to respond, even if it means apologizing. The encounter with Universal Love disarms us, heals us, and fills us with new life-giving energy. It makes us more compassionate, more loving, more present, and more nonviolent to others. The act of surrender into Universal Love helps us be loving, even toward those who are not loving or kind to us. The experience can help us return to Universal Love and send us out all over again, more centered in love. Then, as we go through our day, we learn to stop periodically, sometimes literally, take a deep breath, and connect again with Universal Love. As we do that, we surrender all over again and become living, breathing, acting extensions of Universal Love.

Of course, one could say, "Hey, I meditate, I pray, I seek God—but I still want to explode when someone steps on my toes or pushes my buttons." That, too, is normal. The point is that daily meditation grounds us in Universal Love and reminds us to keep surrendering throughout the day. There will always be obstacles. What we are doing is learning to surrender each one to God, to Universal Love, so that we don't react negatively but rather do God's will and respond with love and compassion, and so make peace.

But the problem for me is that the words *love* and *peace* have been coopted by the culture of fear, hatred, selfishness, and war. Everyone is for love—we love our cars, our TVs, our coffee, but not necessarily the poor, the marginalized, our enemies. Everyone is for peace. The generals and nuclear-weapons manufacturers tell us they are all for peace, though it might cost millions of lives to achieve it. That's why so many of us are turning back to the clumsy word of Gandhi and Dr. King—*nonviolence*—to understand what it means to be surrendered to Universal Love, the God of Peace.

The original word that Gandhi used for nonviolence was *ahimsa*, which means "do no harm in thought, word, or deed." That is what it means to live in surrender to God and to become an extension of Universal Love. As Gandhi learned, God's will for the entire human race is that we practice nonviolence, that our love and peace are so sincere, true, and committed that we renounce all harm, all killing, all war, and give our lives so that everyone lives in the fullness of love and peace.

The goal, I said, is to become totally nonviolent so that you can respond instinctively with nonviolence, no matter what happens at any moment, so that you become deep down the person you want to be—an extension of universal love, a peacemaker. It helps if you spend quality time with your God so that you get regularly disarmed and recentered in God's love and peace. Without that consistent practice, it's easy to get lost in your own self-centeredness and ego. The minute someone does not treat you as you demand or things do not go your way, you get annoyed, frustrated, impatient, resentful, afraid, angry, or even violent. You regress to your inner three-year-old self.

In this case, I said to Will, if you were centered and mindful in the God who loves you and God's spirit of peace, you might have taken a deep breath and said something like, "I feel hurt by those words." You could have used *nonviolent communication*, or *mindful communication*, which uses *I* language to help others know how you feel and what you need, instead of pointing the finger of blame at them ("You did this to me! You're to blame! It's your fault! You're the problem!"). Responding with anger, judgment, and violence, and then walking away, does not resolve the incident but makes it worse. You end up feeling ashamed and guilty.

To avoid guilt and shame, I said, do not respond with the same hurtful words or tone used against you, but do not passively walk away either. Share how it has affected you, if you can. Maybe you will discover that the person did not mean to hurt you but meant something else entirely. If you are not able to speak, you can always pray for that person, forgive the person in your heart, and offer a blessing upon that person, right there on the spot, in your heart. By using creative nonviolent alternative responses, you maintain your peace and help others to reclaim their peace. The more you retain your peace and respond to every occasion with peace, the more God's peace will spread and disarm others.

After this speech I gave Will my copy of Marshall Rosenberg's classic work *Nonviolent Communication*, which should be required reading and practice for every human being. It outlines the various steps and techniques of listening and communicating so that dialogue and relationships can become more nonviolent, reconciling, and loving.

One simple response that often works is to use the word *curious*. It is a nonthreatening word that invites rather than puts down. "I'm curious why you would say that about me?" "I'm curious about how you're feeling that would make you say that?" The word *curious*, as the Buddhist teacher Pema Chödrön suggests, can help open a space for the other to find a place of deeper introspection and realize that he or she was being hurtful toward you or others without your showing any sign of judgment upon the person. Instead, it reveals empathy and compassion, which is the way we want to relate to everyone—and the way we hope others will respond to our mistakes.

A few weeks later Will returned to share another encounter from his workplace. Someone had snubbed him, and this time, instead of barking at the person or retaliating, he talked reasonably with the person in a calm, peaceful voice and left feeling much better. "It works if I stay centered in my breath, and peaceful and calm," he said. "And I found I'm better able to respond like this when I've begun my day in quiet meditation with Universal Love."

Of course, I responded: "I told you so." We both laughed.

❧

The Highest Expression of Humanity's Conscious State

"Devotion to nonviolence is the highest expression of humanity's conscious state," Gandhi once wrote. I shared this quote with Will along with my astonishment at Gandhi's wisdom.

Is Gandhi right? If so, then we have a long way to go, for humanity is thoroughly addicted to violence and to the despair and apathy that come with it, and that global addiction has touched each of us and brought

us to the brink of personal, collective, and global destruction.

On the other hand, if he is right, we have a way out,
a way through, a way forward. Any one of us can try to
develop a higher consciousness of total nonviolence. That
is how we become fully human. As Gandhi explained it,
we seek to "avoid violence in thought, word, and deed";
to non-cooperate with every trace, level, and structure
of violence; and to pursue only truth and love as God
would have us do.

Gandhi showed that if we delve deep within through
meditation and concentration, with the support of community and public service, we can disarm our hearts and
become instruments for disarming our nation and the
world. He spoke of developing "an indomitable will."
Like an athlete who trains for a marathon or an Olympic
race, we train ourselves to let go of violence, to cultivate
nonviolence in every aspect of our lives, and then to go
forward publicly to organize and mobilize others for
a more just, more nonviolent world. We pursue with
indomitable will the willingness to surrender our will
and do only God's will and become instruments of God's
peace and disarmament in the process.

Will immediately latched on to the strategy of practicing "an indomitable will" toward nonviolence and
universal love. It was the approach he took in fitness, and
he realized it was the way he could approach life, only

with a catch—that he would have a steadfast will toward surrendering his will to the will of Universal Love.

In his book *Balancing Heaven and Earth*, Carl Jung's student Robert Johnson writes that we are born "unconsciously conscious" (think of the baby who is fully open to love and joy); that we spend most of our lives "consciously unconscious"; but that the journey and goal of life is to finally become "consciously conscious." That is what Gandhi tried to do, and what he achieved. His life became a spiritual explosion of nonviolence, with glorious social, economic, and political implications for his country, the world, and generations to come.

Full consciousness involves living in the present moment through awakened mindfulness, daily gentleness, heartfelt openness, public service, authentic worship of the God of Peace, and steadfast commitment to the truth. For Gandhi, not a moment of life was to be wasted. Conscious nonviolent living meant experimenting with one's life, with the truth of nonviolence, and with full surrender to God. For Gandhi, that included both relentless inner work toward personal disarmament through prayer, meditation, silence, and study, as well as active public work to end poverty, injustice, and war. In this way he brought the methodology of Jesus in the Gospels onto the modern stage as never before.

This then is the invitation: to devote ourselves to nonviolence, to practice it every day, and to see our ongoing daily practice of nonviolence as a key aspect of our total surrender to the God of Peace. With each nonviolent thought, word, and deed, with each step of nonviolence, we become more fully conscious, more fully human, more fully centered in the peace of God, and more fully surrendered to the God of Peace.

Nonviolence Means Remembering Who We Are

At some point I realized that Will might not have a working definition of nonviolence as I have come to understand it. Many do not grasp the meaning of nonviolence. How *do* we define violence and nonviolence? This is an important question we can revisit and ask one another regularly. We can speak of violence as a physical act of harm, or the expression of mean words toward another, or even an attitude of hostility toward ourselves, creation, and God. We can also recognize our complicity with the systems, structures, and institutions of violence, that range from gun violence, racism, and capital punishment, to militarism, corporate greed, and the predatory policies of multinational corporations that threaten the planet.

But it's even deeper than that. That's why Gandhi spent so much time defining, teaching, and discussing nonviolence. His definition began with a call to avoid injury in thought, word, and deed, but it went on to encompass the universal love and disarming peace of God at work in us, among us, and even through us to foster new cultures of nonviolence.

Over time I have come to understand violence as forgetting who we are. We forget that we are sons and daughters of the God of Peace—that we are brothers and sisters of one another. The minute we forget who we are and who our brothers and sisters are, we diminish ourselves and dehumanize them. Then it becomes possible for us to hurt and kill them, if not deliberately, then through what Pope Francis called a "culture of indifference." They simply don't matter to us.

Violence is a disease of amnesia. Nonviolence is the cure.

Nonviolence, therefore, means striving in every moment to remember who we are: full human beings, brothers and sisters of every other human being, sons and daughters of the Creator God of Peace.

If violence is the social, national, and global act of forgetting ourselves, then nonviolence requires that all of us together try to remember who we are. We awaken to our true selves. We get past the commercials, the money-driven news, the war propaganda, the prejudices, and the grudges that frame our cultures, and we work to create new cultures of inclusivity, openness, nonviolence, justice, and equality. We can all learn the skills and tools to help us remain awake to the truth of our common unity and humanity. That is the journey of every life. We are the infinitely loved children of God, who, because we have surrendered to Universal Love, can become vessels of God's very life and reign of peace here on earth as it is in heaven.

ᔕ

Know Thyself Nonviolently

The adage of the ancient Greeks—*Know thyself*—is another way to begin anew on the path of nonviolence. Not myself as I used to be, not myself as a kid, a teenager, or a young person, but myself right now, with all my current problems, struggles, weaknesses, failings, and brokenness, but also strengths, beauty, hopes, dreams, and joys. The whole package.

Can I take stock and look at myself without judgment or shame and start again the path of healing, inner disarmament, and renewal? Yes. Through meditation, prayer, and practice, I can review my life, work on short-term achievable changes, and set goals for longer-term bigger changes so that I mature into a more whole, loving, and nonviolent person.

In his book *New Seeds of Contemplation*, Thomas Merton described the difference between the false self and the true self and urged us to become our true selves. He said that if we accept our true selves, the deep-down truth of ourselves as we are, and reject our illusions, traps, addictions, and ego projections, we will find an inner peace and joy because we will rediscover our inner goodness and the freedom of being sons and daughters of the God who already loves us.

Most of us, however, have yet to embrace or even seek our true selves. Instead, we cling to various false selves that we think we should or might be, or those created in our minds and hearts by unhealthy patterns of grasping and self-obsession.

As we reflect on ourselves, our habits, our traits, and our journeys—in the safe, sacred space of daily meditation with Universal Love—we can feel a new compassion toward ourselves, let our false illusions fall away, and accept the truth of who we really are. Through this process of contemplative honesty and disarmament, we become better extensions of Universal Love and peace. We enter more fully into God and God's way of nonviolence. God is a mystery, we ourselves are a mystery, and therein lies the journey. We turn within toward our deepest, truest selves and the Universal Love from which we come that we might live as our true selves, as extensions of Universal Love, and then help others reclaim their true selves that someday we might all live in Universal Love and Peace as the sisters and brothers we already are.

Look Deeply Within

Will and I were back at the Blackhorse Café, sipping our decafs and discussing negative feelings such as anger, hostility, and fear. As those emotions occurred, Will was learning how to return to his breath, to recenter himself in Universal Love, and to let those hard emotions go. Surrender it all, I said. Deal with your inner violence nonviolently. I told about him about a beautiful phrase I first heard from Thich Nhat Hanh: when such feelings arise, simply "look deeply within." Seek a compassionate understanding for the reason behind those hard feelings and behaviors; then breathe in peace and breathe out and let it all go, and do the next right thing. I have found this helpful for many years, I told him.

As I practiced "looking deeply within" over time, I understood myself more and more and saw how prone I am to responding selfishly, egotistically, even harmfully. I began to explore the roots of these negative feelings and propensities. And over time, as I surrendered myself entirely to the God of Peace, I felt the roots of my ego, pride, and resentment break off, allowing a new inner peace to take root.

This ongoing inner work of surrender takes me further along the journey of disarmament. It's a journey deeper into total nonviolence—and we always come back to this—total trust in and reliance upon God.

"This is the daily practice of peace," I told Will. "In this way, we learn the fine art of inner disarmament, and when the day comes to stand up publicly, we can march in the streets and speak out publicly for justice and disarmament from an authentic place of peace and universal love. In that way, our public work for peace might bear some lasting fruit. These little moments of breathing in peace and transforming our spirits train us for the bigger moments to come and over the years become a lifetime of breathing peace."

❦

Looking into My Own Violence

To deepen in nonviolence, I suggested, we better look deeply first at our own violence.

If I take the time and study my life, I am ashamed to discover it has been a long journey of violence. As a kid, my brothers and I fought one another, and I happily joined in. Entering the Jesuits, I learned to think of myself as superior to my brothers in the Society and cultivated a deep, inner self-righteousness. Occasionally, in my public lectures on peace, I felt or even expressed anger at people for what I perceived as their hardness of heart, ignorance, or cruelty. I have been mean to those close to me, bullied co-workers, looked down upon others, including the poor and marginalized, supported war and government corruption through apathy and fatalism, turned away from the plight of the poor and done little to improve their lot. I have given in to despair in the face of global violence. In other words, I have not been a channel of peace, love, and nonviolence, but more often than not, a channel of apathy, complicity, cynicism, and indifference. On my worst days I have given in to despair and bitterness and ended up hurting others.

I have cultivated violence in the small details of life, enough to sow the seeds of violence. I have put myself down, hated myself, given up on myself, and, at the same time, been full of myself, brimming with arrogance, pride, narcissism, self-righteousness, and first-world entitlement. To be blunt: I have been comfortable with my complicity in the culture of violence.

What to do? The Twelve Steps of AA offer a guideline. I need to name and repent of my violence. Then, admit my complicity, even my powerlessness in the face of the culture of violence. Then, turn to my Higher Power for help. Then, make amends for the harm I've done others and admit when I've been wrong, ask those I've harmed to forgive me, and forgive all those who have harmed me. Only then will I be able to start life anew each day on the journey of surrender to my Higher Power and into the sobriety of peace and nonviolence. Then I can go forth, serve others, and make peace.

The good news is that gradually I notice new, small victories of nonviolence. I see occasions when I have paused and lingered in God's peace before retaliating with a harsh word, a passive aggressive attitude, or any trace of violence, and learned how to use the tools of nonviolence to refrain from further harm. This daily practice of interior nonviolence along with concrete acts of love, service, and nonviolence toward others, I trust, will bear the good fruit of peace, and allow God's grace to flow freely through me and work through me so that, even in my brokenness, I might become an authentic channel of God's peace.

‿ಎ

The Bottom Line

Narcotics Anonymous requires its members to hold to a bottom line: not to take drugs anymore. Alcoholics Anonymous requires its members also hold to a bottom line: not drink alcohol anymore. The theory is that the Twelve Steps teach you how to live one day at a time so that you no longer need to take drugs or drink yourself to death.

The bottom line of being peaceful, loving, and nonviolent in a world of violence is equally stark and challenging: never harm any living being in thought, word, or deed ever again.

I think this is the bottom line for being human, for practicing the spiritual life, and for living in peace: do no harm. We try with all our attention never to hurt ourselves, another person, or another creature. If every human being pursued this bottom line, the days of violence and war would end.

If we set this goal of strict nonviolence as the bottom line of our day-to-day behavior, then we have our work cut out for us. We need the God of Peace and Universal Love to help us because we are helpless before the world's violence and all the ways we have internalized it. We need others. We need a community of peacemaking friends to support and encourage us in this inner work of disarmament and surrender to the God of Peace. And we need a new daily rhythm of prayer, study, and action that can help us live nonviolently.

By adhering to our bottom line of total nonviolence, we set strict boundaries for our thoughts and words, our behavior and actions, and the entire way we look upon life and what we do. Everything now is lived and understood within the framework of nonviolence. Once we step into the boundaries of nonviolence—that is, into the fullness of surrender to the God of Peace—then it becomes possible for Universal Love to grow and bloom in us so that we radiate it out to others. Just imagine this: if we remain within the boundaries of nonviolence all our lives, then God might use us to disarm and transform the world.

❧

Being Nonviolent to Myself

In our initial conversations about nonviolence, I noticed that Will often mentioned his failings. Occasionally, he judged himself harshly rather than practicing compassion toward himself. That only made things worse. How well I knew this from my own experience! So it was with humility and gratitude that I could say, "To be nonviolent to others, you need to be nonviolent to yourself."

How can I advocate nonviolence for others and our world and still cultivate violence within me? I cannot be nonviolent to others while continuing old patterns of violence toward myself.

So then, the question becomes: How can I be more nonviolent to myself?

I pledge to try every day to be gentle with myself. I will offer compassion to myself. I will give myself a break and let myself off the hook. In doing so, I will be better able to give others a break and let everyone else off the hook. I will take time for compassionate self-care. In this way I make peace with myself, make friends with myself, and treat myself nonviolently. I practice the peace and nonviolence I wish to see in others.

As I have tried to do this, I have slowly discovered the obvious: it feels better to be peaceful within. Compassion toward myself creates a safe place where I can actually change. When I'm not fending off judgment and anger—even toward my own self—I am freer to let go of violent ways, giving up the anger, fear, and resentment. I like being at peace. I desire to be at peace with others.

If making peace with myself helps me feel better, enjoy life, and serve others better, then why linger in old habits? Perhaps I am so well trained in selfishness and violence that I fear taking the leap into some new way of being, even though the evidence proves that there is a much better way to live. That is why I keep pursuing inner peace. In fact, I work harder for interior peace than I work for peace publicly in the world. I realize that to be a strong towering oak tree of peace and comfort to others, my roots need to dig deep and stretch even farther down into the hidden ground of Universal Love within. When I am gentle, peaceful, and nonviolent toward myself, I find it is easier to be gentle, peaceful, and nonviolent to others.

Confessing and Apologizing
for the Harm I Have Done

The Twelve Steps suggest that we admit our helplessness before our addiction—whether to drugs, alcohol,
ego, violence, or money—then turn to our Higher
Power, make amends, and embark on a new journey
toward sobriety. If we are addicted to violence as a
species, then we need to confess our addiction to violence, turn to our Higher Power for help with inner
and global disarmament, and start the long road toward
sobriety, toward living nonviolently and creating a culture of nonviolence.

One of the key steps in our recovery from violence
toward a more peaceful life and world occurs when we
recognize, name, and confess the harm we have done to
other human beings and to creation, both in our personal
lives and through our participation in the structures of
violence and injustice. As we own up to the harm we
have done, we can begin the long process of apologizing
to those we have hurt and asking for their forgiveness in
concrete, specific gestures toward making amends and
offering restitution and reconciliation. Salvation from
violence begins the day we wake up, surrender ourselves
fully to the God of Peace, renounce our violence and
selfishness, and are no longer defensive. Instead, from

now on, we say to all those we have harmed: "I was wrong. I'm sorry. I apologize."

In particular, we need to name our complicity with systemic injustice and global violence. We white people, for example, need to confess our racism. We men need to confess our sexism. We wealthy people need to confess our privilege, entitlement, classism, and greed. We North Americans need to confess the horrors we have wreaked upon the world's poor, the Indigenous, the earth, the creatures, the air, and the oceans. The deeper we look within, the more we begin to see our shadow side and our complicity in the social sin of national and global violence. Reparation, restitution, and active reconciliation become a new part of our spiritual lives, as we move from inner, personal, and interpersonal nonviolence into social, national, and global nonviolence and the work of global peacemaking. When our nation finally wakes up to the wisdom of social nonviolence and sets up Truth and Reconciliation Commissions about European colonialism, genocide against the Indigenous peoples, plantation economics, slavery, segregation, Hiroshima and Nagasaki, Vietnam, Central America, Iraq, Afghanistan, corporate greed, and fascism, then we as a people will have turned the corner.

Forgiving Everyone Who Ever Hurt Us

Over time, during our conversations on the connection among surrender, meditation, and nonviolence, Will and I shared a bit of the various ways we had each been hurt. One thing I could say for sure: we all gather wounds throughout life. People treat us badly, we endure tragedy and loss, friends betray us, the list goes on. My own experience taught me a cornerstone practice, I told him one day: "If we want to plumb the depths of inner nonviolence, we have to deal with our resentments. This is a key source of our violence. We have to recognize our resentments and figure out how to let them go; otherwise, they will eat away at us and destroy us."

I have been nursing resentments and grudges for decades, so I am something of an expert on the topic. I have spent decades letting go of resentments toward my relatives, toward Jesuit superiors who hurt me, and toward peace activists who were mean to me. I noticed how my resentments hardened like barnacles on my heart. Instead of loving others freely in peace, my heart at times has grown cold, stony, and bitter. These festering resentments block my progress along the way of surrender and nonviolence. They prevent me from opening into universal love and compassion. Resentment is one of the biggest obstacles for each one of us, and most of us do not even realize how profoundly we hold on to our resentments, our lack of forgiveness, and how those dynamics continue to harm us.

In her book *The Hiding Place*, Corrie ten Boom, the celebrated Dutch Christian woman who, along with her sister, hid Jews from the Nazis in a special room built into the walls of their house, put it this way: "To forgive is to set a prisoner free, and to discover the prisoner was you."

I do not want to live with resentment anymore. It's not worth it. It allows an old hurt to just keep hurting me. It's too great a burden to carry. The only way forward then is to let my resentments go, one by one. So, I center myself in the peace and quiet of meditation, enter the presence of the God of Peace, and turn over to God all my resentments, grudges, and hurts. I put them all into God's hands. In their place, I ask for the gift of God's peace to dwell within me.

To live in universal love and nonviolence we have to forgive everyone who ever hurt us. Of course, this does not happen with the wave of a wand. Yet the long road to genuine forgiveness and true inner peace has to begin somewhere. It starts with a first step and continues as we *practice* forgiving, praying repeatedly for the ones who hurt us, every day, for many years, until that new day when we enter the freedom of true forgiveness. Here is a mantra we might use:

I forgive everyone who ever hurt me.
May everyone I have hurt forgive me.
May the God of Peace whom I have hurt
    forgive me.
May everyone forgive everyone every-
    where, and may the God of Peace forgive
    us all.
May the God of Peace and Universal Love
    reign supreme over me and everyone
    from now on.

Living Every Moment in the
Presence of the God of Peace

A life of total nonviolence means living every day, every moment, every second in the presence of the God of Peace. We try to live and breathe in the Holy Spirit at all times. We try to become so surrendered to God that we radiate God's peace, and if we keep going forward in God's way of creative nonviolence, we can become a force of God's universal love and disarming nonviolence for the whole world.

"That's impossible," Will said with a laugh.

I thought about that and tried to put it another way. "We're not talking about spiritual perfection," I said, "but daily spiritual progress on the path of peace, love, and nonviolence. Dr. King used to tell his friends, just keep going forward on the way."

Yes, it sounds impossible to live every second in the presence of God. It is impossible by our own efforts and will power. But when we surrender to the God of Peace that means trusting ourselves to God's boundless compassion and unconditional love with the confidence that God will use as instruments of God's peace.

As people of nonviolence, we strive to do more than just refrain from hurting others. We try to love everyone, be nonviolent to everyone, and make peace with everyone and all creation. But we are helpless and powerless to do this on our own, so we surrender ourselves to God, and, in essence, join our lives to God's life-giving movement and action in the world.

But nothing will change if we do not change ourselves and participate in God's disarmament of us. As we consistently work on improving and disarming ourselves, and attend to our daily surrender, then God can more freely use us for God's desire for peace with justice.

✑

Every Human Being Is My Sister and Brother

I gave Will a copy of one of my favorite books, *Gandhi the Man* by Eknath Easwaran, which includes essays, photos, and quotes. Gandhi explained the meaning, purpose, and vision of life within the framework of active nonviolence and pointed toward a peaceful way forward for us all. Reflecting on the life of the nonviolent Jesus, Gandhi concluded that we are all one, that we are all united, that all life is sacred, that we are all sisters and brothers, all children of one loving God.

And because every human being is our sister or brother, we can never hurt any human being ever again. We would never want to hurt our sisters and brothers. We want to love them, serve them, help them, and enjoy the peace of life with them.

In a world of eight billion sisters and brothers, all of us stuck in some mysterious individual and global addiction to violence, the task of nonviolence is hard, even near impossible. Certainly, on our own, it is impossible. But if we surrender to the God who created us and recognize everyone as our brother or sister, the task becomes easier.

I've concluded that Gandhi's vision of universal nonviolence offers the best way to make sense of life and reality, even our theology and spirituality of peace. Yet this ultimate universal vision is ignored by the nations and media. We can't expect governments and corporations to move the world toward peace, but we can remember this vision of God's global, universal family, surrender to God and God's vision, and do what we can as Gandhi did to pursue that vision and make it a reality.

∽

Experimenting with Nonviolence

Gandhi suggests that we approach the question of nonviolence as a scientific experiment. This is what I've tried to do for forty years, I told Will. What would happen if you were nonviolent in this situation? If you did not offer a sharp, angry response? If you backed off, kept quiet, drove more peacefully, and acted less aggressively? If you were positive to those who are negative to you, if you did not take the bait and let the usual people in your life trigger you and push your buttons? If you got off the couch, attended local organizing meetings and got involved in grassroots movements for justice and disarmament?

What would happen if you did not continue your same old violent habits and ways? If you non-cooperated with violence at every level, within yourself, your family, your church, your community, your country, and the world? What would happen if you started to experiment with nonviolence in the little things and the big things, in the tiny moments and bigger experiences of life?

As you experiment with nonviolence in both your daily life and socially in grassroots movements for positive social change, you discover that Dr. King was right: nonviolence is power. The culture of violence, injustice, and war tells us that we are powerless, that there is nothing we can do, that we should give up in anger, fear, and despair and do nothing. But as we experiment with nonviolence, we find that it works and that we have more power than we ever dreamed. We can even begin to understand Gandhi's outrageous statement that the nonviolence of people power is more powerful than all the weapons of the world combined.

Violence doesn't work. Violence in response to violence only leads to further violence. Nonviolence breaks the spiral of violence and transforms even the worst situation into an occasion for peace and hope. This peacemaking, truth-seeking methodology is ultimately how positive social change comes about, including the end of slavery in Britain, segregation in the United States, apartheid in South Africa, and Communism in the Soviet bloc.

I shared with Will a favorite passage from *A Testament of Hope: The Essential Writings of Martin Luther King, Jr.* "The ultimate weakness of violence is that it is a descending spiral begetting the very thing it seeks to destroy," Dr. King writes. "Instead of diminishing evil, it multiplies it. Through violence you may murder the liar, but you cannot murder the lie, nor establish the truth. Through violence you murder the hater, but you do not murder hate. In fact, violence merely increases hate. Returning violence for violence multiplies violence, adding deeper darkness to a night already devoid of stars. Darkness cannot drive out darkness; only light can do that. Hate cannot drive out hate; only love can do that."

King concludes: "If you succumb to the temptation of using violence in the struggle, unborn generations will be the recipients of a long and desolate night of bitterness, and your chief legacy will be an endless reign of meaningless chaos. In spite of temporary victories, violence never brings permanent peace. . . . Nonviolence is a powerful and just weapon which cuts without wounding and ennobles the one who wields it. It is a sword that heals."

As we experiment with the truth, power, and the creative alternatives of nonviolence, we begin to understand nonviolence as the methodology of the God of Peace and imagine new ways in which we could be more peaceful and loving. As we surrender ourselves to the God of Peace and try to do God's will of nonviolence, we become Gandhian social scientists who discover new breakthroughs of peace, even when all hope seems lost.

My Neanderthal Nature

"As soon as I finish my morning meditation and walk out the front door, I turn back into a Neanderthal,"Will told me on the phone the other day.

"No problem," I said. "That happens to all of us. But at least now you notice it. Now you can use your tools to reclaim and maintain your true nature as a sane, non-violent, selfless, compassionate person, an extension of Universal Love. You know how to do this!" I told him. "You have the tools. You know that your Neanderthal ways do not work, that you can do better and that deep down you want to. All you have to do is take a deep breath, recenter yourself mindfully in the present moment, surrender all over again, and live in the spirit of your meditation. It is a daily journey that gets easier over the years.

"But if that doesn't work, no problem. You don't have to beat yourself up, give in to despair, or say it's impossible. You just have to surrender all over again to Universal Love. You give your Neanderthal ways over to Universal love and say, 'You deal with it.' Then, you go about your business in the present moment, relaxed and at peace knowing that Universal Love has got your back."

Later, I suggested, he might ask himself, "Why do I prefer my Neanderthal side and not my peaceful, mindful, surrendered self in Universal Love? Why do I always fall back into my old habits? Remember, you have a lifetime of practice living in your old Neanderthal ways, and this new path is still new, and it too requires a lifetime of practice, so you are on a journey, one day at a time."

And I told Will, "I often see myself in terms of good Doctor Jekyll, who turns at night into the violent Mr. Hyde," although I only knew the Abbot and Costello comedy version. "Life has been a long, slow journey of taming Mr. Hyde and claiming my true nonviolent self."

I continued: "You cannot do it all on your own; you need help and support to live as your true self. Otherwise, if it's just you, then the ego is in charge all over again. Life is a journey in humility and trust in God, daily letting go of the ego and control, surrendering ourselves and every outcome to God, reaching out to friends for guidance and support, using the tools you have learned, practicing selfless service of others, and deepening in conscious unity with all humanity and creation as God's beloved community.

"It is about aligning our hearts, our spirits, and our will to Universal Love. No matter what happens, even when the bottom falls out, we will still trust and hope in Universal Love, even if we feel no emotional consolation.

Indeed, even in the darkest time, we can still know some contentment and inner joy because Universal Love has got our back."

❦

Soft Front, Strong Back

Once, I co-led a retreat on nonviolence with my friend, Buddhist teacher and leader Roshi Joan Halifax, author of *Standing at the Edge* and *Being with Dying.* During the weekend, she spoke about the lifelong "posture" of nonviolence. Most of us live in fear, distrust, and anxiety, she said, ready at any moment for violence. We walk with the posture of violence, which she called, "strong front, soft back." We appear to be tough, defensive, aggressive, ready at a moment's notice to strike back, retaliate, put down, dominate, or hurt others. That aggressive front is artificial, she said. It betrays a "soft back," literally a spineless spirit living in fear and hate.

The posture of nonviolence, on the other hand, features a "soft front, strong back." We are open to all people, she taught us—nonviolent, vulnerable, risking love, kind, hospitable, and compassionate. It takes bravery, courage, faith, and goodwill to stand without weapons, unarmed in a world armed to the teeth, ready to reach out in love and service. That is why nonviolence requires a strong back, she continued. We have backbone. We have an inner strength stronger than any violence. We rely on the God of Peace, we know who we are, we see everyone as a sister or brother; we are grounded in Mother Earth and hold out our palm in a gesture of universal love toward everyone. We can be bold without a trace of violence. We walk tall, at one with humanity and creation, in the Holy Spirit of Peace and Universal Love, open to one and all, but as solid as a redwood tree.

Anyone can be spineless, Roshi said. Develop a backbone, she suggested, and you can stand up to anyone in the force and power of truth, love, vulnerability, and compassion, sharing the gift of peace far and wide.

❦

The Reverse Gratitude List

The other day Will texted me to see how I was doing. "Great," I responded, "and you?"

"Hanging in there, surviving," he answered. This seemed unusual since he was just back from living in the Bahamas and working at a resort for nearly a year, and about to fly off in a few days to New Zealand to hike and camp for several weeks and go bungee jumping (despite my humorous objections).

"What's happening?" I asked.

"I spent the whole weekend helping my father set up some new technology and felt frustrated the whole time," he texted back.

I knew just the solution, an important tool I learned from one of my many spiritual guides: the ol' reverse-gratitude list. In this prayer we thank the God of Peace for the things we are not grateful for! For everything that's going wrong, and for the opportunity, through surrender and grace, to draw closer to God and transform even these situations deeper into love and peace! It's best to write it down and pray through it sincerely, I was taught.

"Here is a little prayer for you," I texted back:

Thank you, God of Peace and Universal Love, for this opportunity to set up new technology for my father; for the chance to be with him and return the loving kindness and generosity he's always shown me; for the chance to move through my frustration to patience, humility, and unconditional love; for the opportunity most of all to grow in awareness of your loving presence here with me as I try to be an extension of your loving kindness. Through this experience you show me how patient, kind, generous, and understanding you are with me, when you could have been far more than frustrated. Thank you for all your loving kindness toward me. Help me share that loving kindness, patience, and compassion with everyone I meet from now on, starting with my beloved father.

Will thanked me and generously agreed. This practice turns our self-will upside down and exposes our selfishness. He is on a journey with Universal Love, so I knew he might find this intentional act, "the reverse gratitude," as a door into deeper freedom, patience, compassion, love, and peace.

∾

Radical Letting Go, Radical Acceptance

My friend and teacher Father Daniel Berrigan talked regularly over the course of many decades about letting go. It was for him the key to the spiritual life, the language of surrender to God. Once he was a world-famous poet and peacemaker, a leading figure against the Vietnam War and nuclear weapons, featured on the cover of *Time* magazine and nominated repeatedly for the Nobel Peace Prize. He would reflect quietly on the necessity of letting go of one's ego, plans, possessions, pride, and very self. Every day he said he let go more and more. I knew him closely for over thirty years and watched him mellow in spirit but remain as committed as ever to the truth of peace and nonviolence and therefore resistance to the culture of violence and war.

By the time he was in his eighties, he was very much at peace and free. He didn't cling to anything. He spent his nineties almost entirely bedridden but at peace, smiling, pleasant, fun to be around, happy to see people. He never had cancer, a heart attack, or even surgery. He never even took a pill, much to the dismay and astonishment of his Manhattan doctors. When he died a week before his ninety-fifth birthday, on April 30, 2016, he slipped away gently and quietly, completely at peace. He had no baggage because he had long ago let go. He was free in peace.

The life of nonviolence invites us to a radical letting go, to a daily surrender into universal love and eternal peace. As we take a deep breath and let go of whatever we cling to, we discover some new depth of freedom.

But there is an odd flip side that comes with radical letting go, which is radical acceptance. While we let go, we also accept everything that happens to us, such as old age, decline, diminishment, suffering, and impending death. We accept it all in a spirit of love, compassion, and peace. We have long ago surrendered our lives to the God of Peace, so by now we accept what happens to us as a gift from the God of Peace.

If we dare let go and accept everything, both at the same time, in a highwire act of peace, we will experience the fruits of the surrendered life and transcend every selfish, egocentric inclination of pride, resentment, anger, or violence and know the heights and depths and length and breadth of God's own peace. In the end we are accepting peace as God's personal gift to us, an eternal gift of true inner freedom, love, and joy that no one can take from us. In the process we become living extensions of God's universal love without our even knowing it.

∾

Befriending Our Fears

One day at the Blackhorse Café, Will and I got talking about our fears. Then and there we did a timed writing practice about them. I told him how impressed I was at twenty-two to read that Gandhi professed sixteen vows as a young man, including vows of nonviolence, truth, poverty, and respect for all world religions, and even a vow of fearlessness. This was particularly difficult for him because he lived in terror for most of his childhood. He could barely sleep at night when he was a boy because he feared the possible dangers that lurked around him. Through meditation, study, community, and relentless practice, he learned that love banishes all fear, that as we deepen in nonviolence and trust in the God of Peace, we need not fear because God is on our side, truth is on our side, universal love is on our side, indeed, our very survival is already guaranteed.

Throughout his instructions on love and nonviolence, Jesus repeated to his students this one maxim: Do not be afraid. He wanted them strong in faith and love; steady in their mission of creative nonviolence; and eager to go forth, serve the poor, and proclaim God's reign of peace as our true home. Such public troublemaking and resistance could only lead to a bloody outcome. But even as he faced harassment, death threats, assassination attempts, betrayal, arrest, trial and execution, the nonviolent Jesus surrendered himself and trusted completely in God.

Will told me some of the things he fears, and I shared my lifelong fear of death. "But there is a way to transcend fear," I said. "That is to move beyond it into a new liminal space of trust and freedom in God. Again, it is a matter of surrendering ourselves to God, letting go of everything and accepting everything, stepping into the light and wisdom of nonviolence, and becoming extensions of Universal Love with open, vulnerable hearts.

"To deal with my fears, I spent years praying over them, letting them go, journaling about them, and stepping into faith in the God of Peace as my security. Over time I felt able to face anything despite my fears. I learned to speak publicly in front of large crowds despite my anxieties. I faced arrest and jail many times for civil disobedience in a spirit of calm and mindfulness.

"I even lived in a refugee camp at the height of El Salvador's civil war in 1985 as death squads roamed the countryside and US bombs dropped every hour before my eyes on the nearby Guazapa mountain," I told him. "The Salvadoran poor taught me how to live in faith, hope, and love, and very quickly I moved from fear to peace and joy. They were free interiorly and practiced an exuberant love for one another that was contagious. They had nothing except one another and their faith and hope in the God of Peace. I began to feel the same thing. That is why I know it is possible to get beyond fear.

"We need not be afraid. We can stand and walk in peace, hope, and love, trusting that the God of Peace will protect us, come what may, including arrest, jail, war, and death. Once we befriend our fears, they start to evaporate and we discover an interior freedom that no one can take from us. Fearless, creative nonviolence is our path to liberation into Universal Love. We can trust that all will be well."

I have a secret name for this practice of fearlessness, nonviolence, and universal love: Getting ready for resurrection.

∽

The Practice of Affirmation

Over the years Will and I often returned to the practice of meditation, surrender, and nonviolence, noticing the various patterns in our day-to-day lives that arose like obstacles on our pilgrimage. We each could see them now because in meditation we began to notice how the mind works. In surrendering to God we noticed how our willfulness works against us. And in our mindful nonviolence, we noticed the cracks that could unleash the unholy spirit of violence.

As we deepen in surrender and nonviolence, I told Will, we notice when negative thoughts arise and we learn how to drop them. First, we let go of any negative thoughts toward ourselves. If we ever hear that inner voice putting ourselves down, whispering negativity such as "you're no good," "you're a terrible person," "you should hate yourself," you learn to stop, surrender those negative thoughts to God, and breathe in God's peace. Those who struggle with low self-esteem learn to practice positive, nonviolent self-talk. In those moments we intentionally tell ourselves, "I'm a good person," "I'm a lovable and loving person," "I do good in the world," "I am loved by the God of Universal Love." We can voice these affirmations throughout our day to break through our negativity and redirect our inner disposition and feelings toward our loving God and the positivity of God's peace.

Likewise, when negative thoughts toward others arise, we stop, pause, surrender them to God, breathe in that spirit of peace and nonviolence, and replace them with positive thoughts toward others. If we ever hear that negative voice within, we surrender these thoughts to God and ask God to take them away, and immediately offer a heartfelt prayer for those others. We bless them and feel compassion, empathy, and love for them, and wish for them every good blessing that we would wish for ourselves and our loved ones.

I have met many people who radiate heartfelt love through positive affirmation. One of these was the late Fred Rogers, star of the PBS children's show *Mister Roger's Neighborhood*. I met Fred at the funeral of our mutual friend Father Henri Nouwen. We both read the prayers of the faithful and after the beautiful mass, we spoke and I told him about my work for peace. He immediately asked me for my phone number, called me the next day, and we talked or wrote regularly for the next six years until his death.

On several occasions, while I was living in New York City, he would invite me to join him at some public function, and I would watch him with awe and wonder. Every single time I was with him he said something positive to me. He was always encouraging me. It was only after his death that I realized I had never known anyone else who did that. He practiced affirming others as a way of life, as his way of universal love and intentional peacemaking. He lived his entire life affirming and encouraging every person he met. Because of this, it always felt good to be with him. You felt better about yourself in his presence.

"I believe that appreciation is a holy thing—that when we look for what's best in a person we happen to be with at the moment, we're doing what God does all the time," Fred once wrote. "So, in loving and appreciating our neighbor, we're participating in something sacred."

His practice of positive energy, affirming and encouraging others, and universal compassion changed my life. He saw the infinite goodness within everyone, and told people how good they were. Because he was so widely known, many of us had the experience of being loved and affirmed by him. He set a powerful example of how to transcend every form of negativity, judgmentalism, cynicism, despair, darkness, resentment, anger, and violence, turning them into love, compassion, nonviolence, and peace.

As we surrender to the God of Peace and cultivate interiorly God's peace, we notice the goodness and beauty within everyone, and like Fred Rogers, become a force of affirmation and encouragement to every person we meet. In that way, as we encourage one another, we spend our days in peacemaking peace

∽

The Potential to Become Nonviolent Is within Everyone

"I can't be totally nonviolent," Will said to me on the phone one day. "It's just not possible."

That's what we all think, what we have all been taught to believe by the culture of violence and war: it is not possible to practice total nonviolence. Deep down, we are all brainwashed after thousands of years by the culture of violence. There is no hope that we could become truly nonviolent, truly loving, selfless and compassionate to ourselves, all others, and creation.

Our addiction to violence runs so deep that we cannot achieve the sobriety of nonviolence, we think. But that's the whole point of the Twelve Step movement: while we will always be an addict, we can become sober through our inner work, meditation, surrender to our Higher

Power of Peace, community support, and living strictly one day at a time. If we want to be nonviolent, we can. It's a lifelong journey, a way of life, a spiritual practice as well as a daily discipline. It takes surrender to God's will, but it is doable. It's not about becoming perfect or successful. Those words do not appear in the vocabulary of peace. Rather, it's a progressive journey toward ever-deepening nonviolence into the God of Peace until we are subsumed in Universal Love and Peace.

That's why I think we should all just see ourselves as members of "Violence Anonymous," violent people who surrender to our higher power, the God of Peace; admit our helplessness; ask for help and strength; make amends to those we have hurt; work with others to live a daily sober life of nonviolence, kindness and peace; and in this new one-day-at-a-time surrendered life, serve humanity and creation as peacemakers, trying to end conflict, violence, and war in order to welcome God's reign of peace.

"I have not the shadow of a doubt than any man or woman can achieve what I have, if he or she would make the same effort and cultivate the same hope and faith," Gandhi said toward the end of his life.

If total nonviolence is not only the highest form of human consciousness but the only practical political and spiritual solution left for humanity, why waste our time on anything less worthy? Isn't this the noblest pursuit we can undertake? Even if we fail, the effort itself is a great victory. We may never achieve total nonviolence, but we can surely move closer to it and discover the freedom of God's peace that comes within the boundaries of nonviolence. As Gandhi said, "Full effort is full victory."

And so, I kept teaching Will and myself: "Surrender everything, every day, every moment to the God of Peace, be grateful for the blessings in your life, and allow yourself to be transformed into an extension of Universal Love, to be taken and used and fashioned into someone you could never become on your own—a servant of humanity and creation, a peacemaker, a light to the world in all its darkness, a vessel of Universal Love, compassion, and peace.

༄

Prayer

*May I Surrender to You and Walk
in Your Peace and Universal Love*

God of Peace,
Thank you for all the blessings of life, love,
    and peace that you give me and all my
    sisters and brothers and all of creation.

Give me the grace to live within the boundaries of nonviolence;

That I may never harm myself or anyone or
any sentient being in thought, word, or
deed ever again;

That I may forgive everyone who ever hurt
me;

That I might apologize, admit my wrongs,
and make amends to all those I have
hurt; and

That I might do your will of nonviolence
and let your Holy Spirit of Universal
Love reign supreme within me throughout my life, that I might deepen in your
peace and love and spread your way and
wisdom of peace, love, and nonviolence
far and wide among people everywhere.

May I always live within the boundaries of
your nonviolence, one day at a time, and
grow in your peace and love and, in doing so, serve you and all humanity and all
creation, from now on. Amen.

Part Three

⚬

Becoming a Channel
of God's Peace in a
Peaceless World

I AM CONVINCED that contemplation is a political act of the highest value, implying the riskiest consequences to those taking part. Union with God leads people, who are then in a sense charged with moral responsibilities that often lead to legal jeopardies—to resistance against false, corrupting, coercive, imperialist policies. The saints were right: their best moments were on the run, in jail, at the edges of "respectable society."

—DANIEL BERRIGAN

THE BEST WAY to find yourself is to lose yourself in the service of others.

—MOHANDAS GANDHI

WE REPEAT: THERE is nothing we can do but love, and dear God—please enlarge our hearts to each other, to love our neighbor and to love our enemy as well as our friend.

—DOROTHY DAY

WE DON'T LIVE for ourselves. We live for others.

—RICHARD ROHR

Taking the Leap of Faith

Fast forward several years. Will spent the pandemic years working as a trainer and a sports coordinator at several vacation resorts. When he had enough, he flew home for a few days, and we met at the Blackhorse Café on several afternoons to drink coffee, talk, and write. Then he headed off on a long dreamed of vacation to New Zealand to hike, and on to Bali to meet his girlfriend. When he landed in Auckland, he flew to the South Island for several day-long hikes in the mountains overlooking Queenstown, which have some of the most majestic views in the world.

He texted me a video of him bungee jumping off a makeshift platform high above a mountain gorge, with some kind of elastic cord attached to him, straight down into oblivion. I found it terrifying. The assistant counts down, and then the jumper dives head first off the ledge straight down some thirty stories until the bungee cord catches him and he bounces back up. That's all the video showed. Later, he told me he had ridden up the mountain in a bus with a dozen others, all of them terrified of the jump but determined to do it, and he spent the long drive encouraging them all to stay calm, mindful, and focused. When his turn came, he breathed deeply, remained steady, centered, and focused, then jumped into the void, trusting that he would be fine, knowing that he was safe, even free from fear, exhilarated by the experience.

For him, it was a metaphor of surrendering to Universal Love.

A few weeks later, back at the Blackhorse Café, he announced his news. While hiking alone in the mountains of Ben Lomond on the South Island, he was "hit by a ton of bricks," he said. He saw a Medivac helicopter fly over the mountain range and said to himself, "That's what I should be doing." He told me that sometimes in meditation and in nature he feels the presence of Universal Love like chills running down his spine, and he felt those indescribable otherworldly chills at that moment, there in the midst of those mountains. He knew to the core of his being what he would do with the rest of his life: he would become a paramedic and spend his life saving and rescuing suffering people in extreme crisis, and in doing so, he would fulfill his vocation to be an extension of Universal Love. He had found his vocation, he said.

I was astounded. I would never have predicted this decision. One minute he was a personal trainer at the local gym and the sports coordinator at a luxury resort in the Caribbean, and now he was determined to give his life in service to Universal Love by spending every day of his life saving lives. With that, he applied to EMT school, threw himself full time into his studies, graduated at the top of his class, and before I knew it, was racing down the highways of Los Angeles at all hours of the night driving an ambulance and quite literally saving lives. He would call with astonishing stories, and I could only marvel at the transformation that had occurred because he had surrendered himself to Universal Love and pledged to do not his own will, but the will of Universal Love. I encouraged him, and we pledged to keep on surrendering ourselves to Universal Love, the God of Peace, come what may.

His stories were incredible, and too many to recite. Within days, he was attending to elderly people who had fallen, young people strung out on drugs and alcohol who had hurt themselves, and victims of car crashes, freak accidents, and unexplainable medical emergencies. Then one night he and his partner pulled up just after a drive-by shooting. Three men in their twenties had been sitting on the front step of a house talking peacefully when a car drove by and the people inside it opened fire. It may have been some kind of demonic gang initiation, where novices are ordered to kill innocent bystanders. None of the victims died, but all of them were shot multiple times.

Will found himself attending to the worst hit victim. He was covered in blood and in pain, so he stopped the bleeding and eventually got him on a stretcher. Will later said that every aspect of his training, including his practice of deep breathing, mindfulness, concentration, trust, and surrender, kicked in. He concentrated all his effort, got this man to the hospital, and helped saved the poor guy's life. Without my friend's steady, speedy, efficient effort, he would have bled out.

"I was very grateful afterward," Will said, "but then I remembered that as I bandaged him and saw an open hole, my own hands started shaking so hard that I put the tape on wrong. I had to take a deep breath, and bandage him all over again. I have much more to learn."

There is nothing scarier or more stressful than being an on call EMT ambulance driver and technician covering all of Los Angeles at nighttime, he said. "I was afraid during my first days, and I was surrendering my fears by name over and over and remembering to breathe. I never know what I'm walking into, and sometimes a wave of anxiety hits me, and again, I surrender it all to Universal Love. Very soon, even in the direst situation, I felt there was nowhere else I'd rather be. My mind wasn't wandering. I was fully present and glad to be of service."

Within days he came face to face with the reality of death, and he seemed to mature by decades. Every time he went to work as a first responder, he would face the frailty, fragility, and mortality that we ignore. Soon he was facing death on an almost daily basis, and that meant he quickly had to face his own mortality and choose each day to believe and trust in life and in the ways and wisdom of Universal Love.

His most difficult call came just a few months down the road. He was used to the basics by then, and well respected by the paramedics he found himself working with. He was still an entry-level EMT ambulance driver and technician who provided immediate services for those in need, but he was learning by leaps and bounds. He entered a house where he found a man in his forties lying unconscious on the floor in the throes of a massive heart attack. The man's children were standing by screaming and crying so hard they were throwing up. Will, his EMT partner, and several firefighters administered CPR and took turns performing chest compressions. Eventually they brought him to the hospital, where he was pronounced dead.

The urgency and shock of the experience traumatized Will. As he looked at the body of the poor man whose face had turned blue, Will thought of all his loved ones who could die just as easily at any moment. For the first time in his life the cold reality and inevitability of death hit him full on, and he understood that he too would one day die. He couldn't sleep for days.

"I felt so close to death," he told me the next day. "I understood my mortality for the first time. I called everyone I love and told them I love them. I suddenly have so much more patience for those I love." For weeks afterward, he meditated on the experience, his own death, the death of his loved ones, and the frailty of life. He felt gratitude for all those he loved and surrendered his fears and his life to Universal Love as never before. "Now that I've come face to face with death, I have a much deeper appreciation of life," he told me a few months after that episode. "Life is short. Now I understand."

∾

The Point Is to Serve

To live fully, nonviolently, and peacefully in a peaceless world is to spend one's life in loving service of all people, all creatures, and all creation. From day one, that's what I told Will I had learned from all my teachers. The catch, however, is that we serve freely and unconditionally—without a trace of the desire to be served in return. We do not seek any reciprocation. We are servants of humanity and creation, pure and simple, and in this way we serve our God the Creator. Not only do we do no harm, but we seek to do only good, and that includes stopping the harm and suffering that others undergo. We not only live and let live, but we live and *help* live.

That's what Cesar Chavez, the legendary founder of the United Farm Workers and apostle of nonviolence, told me shortly before his death. He saw himself as a servant, he said, which meant, that he was at the beck and call of any farmworker in need—morning, noon, and night. His own comfort was not a priority, or even of much interest any more. If a struggling farmworker needed him at 4 a.m. on a Sunday morning, he was there. That's what it means to be a person of nonviolence in a world of poverty, violence, and injustice, he told me. We serve those in need unconditionally. Our lives serve humanity and the nonviolent struggle for justice. "This is what it means to be human."

Martin Luther King, Jr., put it this way: "An individual has not started living until he rises above the narrow confines of his individualistic concerns to the broader concerns of humanity."

❧

Dr. Paul Farmer and the Surrendered Life of Service

When I think of someone who surrendered his life to the God of Peace and ended up giving his entire life, one day at a time, in public service to those in need, I always think of my lifelong friend Dr. Paul Farmer. I always returned to stories about Paul when talking about service with Will. His accomplishments were astounding, but so was his personal spirit and love.

In 1978, while at Duke University, we joined the same crazy, wild fraternity in the center of campus. We both studied hard and partied hard, often till dawn. He was brilliant, on a full scholarship, and number one in his class. Then, in early 1980, roughly about the same time, we both underwent a dramatic spiritual conversion. I instantly felt called one day, Ash Wednesday, 1980, to give my life in unconditional surrender to God as a Jesuit and a priest. He, too, one day, March 24, 1980, felt instantly called to give his life in unconditional surrender to God through service as a medical doctor for the world's poor.

We graduated, and he went on to become a medical anthropologist and physician earning an MD and PhD from Harvard while spending most of his time serving in a clinic in Haiti. The medical professors were so impressed with him that they let him miss many classes, because he knew the material better than they did.

I knew why. Paul had a photographic memory. He was one in a billion. He could read a book and practically recite it back to you. Unlike every other med student in history, he read the chemistry tables and remembered them from then on. Later in life he underwent tests and had his brain waves studied. Unlike the rest of us, whose brains work, say, at 20 percent capacity, Paul's brain was completely turned on, working at nearly 100 percent capacity. All the synapses were working. He was born that way. But what is so amazing is that he surrendered this immense gift and burden to God and the world's poor and became the greatest, most important doctor since Albert Schweitzer.

In 1987, he founded the international non-profit organization Partners in Health, which today has over ten thousand medical doctors serving in some of the poorest places on the planet. He was also named university professor and the chair of the Department of Global Health and Social Medicine at Harvard, and he practiced regularly with patients at the Brigham and Women's Hospital in Boston.

Tracy Kidder's biography of Paul, *Mountains beyond Mountains: The Question of Dr. Paul Farmer—A Man Who Would Cure the World,* told the world about Paul's mission and made him globally famous. The book told of his pioneering work to end rare tuberculosis in Haiti, Peru, and Russia.

But that was only the beginning of his journey. He went on to lead healthcare in Haiti and Rwanda and pioneer community-based treatment that brought state-of-the-art healthcare to some of the poorest people on the planet, proving that it is possible to bring high-quality healthcare to the world's poor. He literally proved his critics—the leading medical journals in the world—wrong, and they admitted it.

I knew Paul for forty-four years and lived with him for three years when we were teenagers.

Years later, we spoke together at St. Paul's Church in Cambridge to a packed crowd. He told them that we used to stay up all night talking about the meaning of life and what we were going to do with our lives. He said I used to read quotes to him from Viktor Frankl's book *Man's Search for Meaning* and ask him, "What are we doing with our lives? What are we going to do with our lives that can be helpful?" That rings true, but I only remember being in awe of him.

He told the story of his dramatic turning-point moment. It occurred on March 24, 1980, the night Archbishop Oscar Romero was assassinated in El Salvador. A handful of students organized a candlelight vigil on the plaza outside the Duke chapel. Paul heard about it and went to it out of curiosity. He said that as he listened to people talk about Romero and joined in the prayers, scales fell from his eyes. He realized that to be a Christian meant one had to be on the side of the poor and marginalized and to serve Christ in those communities.

Paul moved to Haiti and expanded the clinic. I joined the Jesuits and threw myself into work for justice and peace. We stayed in touch, and corresponded periodically. Every step of the way he encouraged me in my efforts to speak out against war, racism, poverty, and nuclear weapons. Keep at it, don't give up, was his constant admonition to me.

That night at Harvard speaking together was a highlight in my life. But the best night of all was his fiftieth birthday, when we threw a party for him to raise funds for Partners in Health. He agreed to the party on condition that it begin with a mass of thanksgiving, led by me. He asked me to preach on Matthew 25. Afterward, we all gave him our blessing. During the party, Bill Clinton and Bill and Melinda Gates spoke. The rock band Arcade Fire performed. There were only one hundred of us at the party in a church basement in Manhattan, and he raised over a million dollars for Partners in Health.

That night I got to meet his mythic Partners in Health cofounders, Ophelia Dahl and Jim Yong Kim, the former president of Dartmouth who later became the head of the World Bank. Jim pressed me with questions. What was Paul like as a kid? I wanted to know how they pulled off creating one of the most important healthcare projects not just in the world, but in history.

Jim got serious and started to cry as he told the story. "Let's start a non-profit organization to bring the highest quality healthcare to the poorest people in the world," Paul said to Jim one day in the 1980s. And then Paul added a caveat. "But there has to be one rule: Everybody

has to be kind. We have to agree to practice unconditional kindness."

I never heard anyone say that before, but I instantly
recognized it as the real Paul Farmer, the one I knew as a
kid. He was always the smartest person around, the fun-
niest person around, the most serious person around—
and the kindest person you'd ever meet. I didn't know
that a global non-profit organization could be founded
and rooted in unconditional kindness. I was shaken by
this story, and once again, by my friend Paul. Suddenly, it
was so clear: this should be the one ground rule for the
church, for every religious institution, for every school
and university and hospital and city, not to mention
every peace, justice, and environmental group: to be a
member, you have to practice unconditional kindness.

Paul was a visionary who reclaimed the imagination,
the new possibilities, of what it means to be human, of
what the world could be. Time and time again he was
told, "You can't do that," and he would always answer,
"Sure we can." And then he did it.

Paul received an endless list of awards for his astonishing accomplishments. I hope the full story of his life will
one day be told. The dean of Harvard Medical School
told me that Paul had spoken at every major medical
school on the planet. "Paul is the most important doctor
in the world. He has changed the way medicine is done
around the whole world." He received scores of honorary

degrees and delivered hundreds of commencement addresses and speeches at global conferences. He was put on the board of directors at Duke, and an annual award was named after him without his even knowing it. But through Partners in Health, he helped save literally millions of lives.

Later I met Dr. Anthony Fauci, who was first Paul's mentor, and then, he said, Paul's student. He said to me, "Well, John, you left Duke and went on to become a priest. Paul left Duke and went on to become St. Francis." I agreed, and we laughed.

I was always amazed at the way he lived and quite speechless in his presence. I remember at one point he described to me how he commuted every Friday. He taught at Harvard for a week; then flew to Haiti for a week; then flew to Rwanda for a week; and then back to Harvard. This routine went on for a decade. At that time his Haitian wife, Didi, and their children lived in Rwanda. I was always stunned and challenged by his witness to rethink how hard I was (or wasn't) working for justice for the poor.

When I heard the news on Monday morning, February 21, 2022, that Paul had died in his sleep in Buturo, Rwanda, on the grounds of a hospital and university that he founded, I was shocked and filled with grief, but not surprised. No one I knew worked harder or gave his life more fully in total service to the poor and marginalized than Paul. He was due to teach a class that morning and never showed up. Turns out, he had spent his last days tending to a cancer patient who was not improving; he could not figure out why, and he was very upset about it.

In *Bending the Arc,* the Netflix film about Paul and Partners in Health, there's a scene in which Paul is working with a patient who has only days to live. The patient says her father is busy building her coffin. Paul puts her on treatment, saves her life, and then casually says to her, "Tell your father to get rid of the coffin. You're not going to need it."

There are so many ways to approach Paul's mythic life. He lived Matthew 25, served Christ in the poor, became a prophet for the poorest of the poor, and was perhaps the greatest doctor in history. But I have always thought of Paul in terms of resurrection. He was a Christ-figure to me even in the 1970s, as I told the crowd at his fiftieth birthday. He was always the life of the party, the one who helped us find the meaning of life, and the one who told the poorest of the poor to get rid of their coffins. He was like Jesus—not only healing the sick but also raising the dead. He took on the powers and forces of the culture of death and brought millions of people back to life.

That's why my friend should not only be canonized as a saint but also named a doctor of the church. He was the doctor who reclaimed the gospel for the poor in an unprecedented way. He did "greater things" even than Jesus, as Jesus said someday someone would.

I take heart knowing that this person who practiced resurrection in the face of death every day of his life lives on with the risen Jesus, and that if we surrender ourselves to God, giving our lives in public service of humanity and creation, we will find ourselves getting ready for resurrection. Paul Farmer shows us, like Jesus, that death does not get the last word. Life does.

∽

The Heights and Depths of Universal Love

"The hardest part of my job as an EMT in Los Angeles is tending to patients who are violent, distraught, drunk or on drugs, who need to be restrained," Will tells me over coffee at the Blackhorse Café. "I'm taught to defend myself; I've been trained all my life to respond with violence, but I can't do that now. So, preparing myself for any possible violent situation is a very real thing now in my day-to-day life.

"The other day," he continues, "I was called to help a schizophrenic man who was wildly drunk. We got him in to the ambulance, but halfway to the hospital he announced he didn't want to go the hospital and demanded to be taken downtown. Somehow, he removed the belts, jumped out the back door, and rolled down the street into the traffic.

"We called the fire department and eventually got him to sit on the curb. When the fire truck arrived, he rolled under the ambulance. So, we all picked him up, strapped him onto the stretcher, and restrained him. The firemen left, so my partner and I and a young EMT student with us got back in and headed back to the hospital. Once again the man started screaming, this time saying he was being kidnapped. In particular, he was threatening the student, who was a light-weight young woman. I felt concerned for her and wanted to protect her. I found I was able to de-escalate the situation throughout just by being a calming presence and using my words slowly and carefully.

"Outside the hospital he started screaming again, and by now I was exhausted. I'd tried everything. There was nothing more I could say. We had him on the stretcher, and I sat on the ground beside him, looked him in the eye, said his name, and said quietly and solemnly to him: 'I'm so sorry you are dealing with this, but I promise you I am only here to help you. Please stop yelling. Please help me to help you. Please promise me you'll calm down and go in peacefully.'

"With that, he put out his hand, said 'I promise,' and I shook it. I took him into the hospital with no more problems, and he received good treatment. I had said these words from the start, but after nearly two hours, he was tired too and was able to listen. I have to choose over and over between the safety of the patient and people being victimized by further violence. I have to always be on my game and remain steady and calm.

"I have to learn and grow from every call, every experience. Sometimes, I make a mistake and harp on my mistake, and I have to learn to surrender that. It's so humbling, first, because everyone else has so much more experience, training, and knowledge. Nowadays, whenever I've had a difficult, challenging call, I take it to my meditation and to Universal Love. I express love and gratitude for Universal Love and allow myself to be loved and to feel my feelings, and I surrender everything. Then, I often name the people I love and send love to them. Meditation helps me process the events and move on. Surrendering to Universal Love gives me a physical relief. I know now this is where I am needed the most because I am doing everything I can."

"You're doing great," I tell him. "Keep going forward, keep on surrendering to Universal Love, keep on learning and growing and living in the present moment with Universal Love. It's a great adventure, and you have found your purpose, your vocation, your calling, the meaning of your life."

Nonviolence All the Way

On April 4, 1967, at Riverside Church in New York City, one year to the day before his assassination, Martin Luther King, Jr., publicly condemned the US war in Vietnam in no uncertain terms in one of the greatest speeches of his life. He deliberately connected the dots between the civil rights movement and the burgeoning peace movement to end the war in Vietnam, and he explained how he had to be consistent in his nonviolence for people of color at home and abroad. That meant he had to oppose all injustice, all violence, all oppression, and all killing, everywhere, on all sides, no matter who was doing the oppressing and killing, including his own government. The next day he was roundly criticized by the Johnson administration and the media, as well as people in his own movement, even his closest friends. From the right he was attacked for having the gall to question US foreign policy. From the left he was lambasted for losing focus and dividing the civil rights movement. Nonetheless, he kept up his campaign of peace and gave his life for his stand of consistent, total nonviolence.

One story has always touched me. It was early 1968, and Dr. King was home alone in his house in Atlanta when a childhood friend stopped by to visit. He had become the first African American police officer in Atlanta. They sat down and he launched into a brutal tirade against King's stand for peace. "Why are you speaking out against the Vietnam War?" he began. "You're undoing all the good you have done. You're confusing civil rights with peace. You're ruining everything."

Dr. King listened patiently, and then told his friend, "Why, you've never understood me at all. When I speak about nonviolence, I mean nonviolent all the way." As David Garrow's classic biography of King, *Bearing the Cross*, reports, he went on to say, "Never could I advocate nonviolence in this country and not advocate nonviolence for the whole world. That's my philosophy. I don't believe in death and killing on any side, no matter who's heading it up—whether it be America or any other country. Nonviolence is my stand, and I'll die for that stand."

The friend later said that it wasn't until that moment that he understood Dr. King. He was shocked to realize that Dr. King was serious about nonviolence, and that his nonviolence was total, consistent, and all-encompassing. King's nonviolence meant having nothing to do with death. He had known King since grade school, followed every step of his journey, heard him preach a hundred times at Ebenezer Baptist, and yet it had never occurred to him that nonviolence was a way of life that required total commitment and consistent application across the board. At best, he thought of it as a tactic and strategy for the movement. Now, he knew Dr. King meant business.

This was life or death stuff, he suddenly realized. This was the way of God! Of course, Martin had to speak against the Vietnam War, and all wars.

A few months later Dr. King was dead, but not before making one last declaration of the existential importance of nonviolence. Standing before the packed crowd of thousands of supporters at the Mason Temple in Memphis the night before his death, Dr. King summed up our global predicament: "The choice before us is no longer violence or nonviolence. It's nonviolence or nonexistence."

Nearly sixty years after his assassination, Dr. King's assessment has come true and plays out in the daily headlines. We have rejected his call for total nonviolence, just as most people for centuries have rejected Jesus's call for total nonviolence. Now, the United States and the world are slipping deeper into authoritarianism, oligarchy, white supremacy, even fascism, and we plunge ahead with permanent warfare, unparalleled corporate greed for a handful of billionaires, a nuclear arsenal on hair-trigger alert, and catastrophic climate chaos in droughts, fires, tornadoes, hurricanes, monsoons, and floods. Our violence has grown exponentially and is spiraling out of control as our global addiction to violence, war, and death increases. Indeed, since Dr. King's death, we have consistently opted for violence and even shunned his clumsy word *nonviolence,* as if it were the most dangerous word in the English language. Perhaps it is.

Like his childhood friend, all of us need to learn the shocking truth that Dr. King, like Gandhi and Jesus, meant what he said: nonviolence is the only way forward for us individually, nationally, and globally, and if we each don't choose nonviolence as a way of life, we are doomed to self-destruction. Like Dr. King, we have to come to a new, more mature, consistent wisdom—total nonviolence in every aspect of life.

"Nonviolence is absolute commitment to the way of love," Dr. King taught. "Love is not emotional bash; it is not empty sentimentalism. It is the active outpouring of one's whole being into the being of another. . . . At the center of nonviolence stands the principle of love. To retaliate with hate and bitterness would do nothing but intensify the hate in the world. Along the way of life, someone must have sense enough and morality enough to cut off the chain of hate. This can be done only by projecting the ethics of love to the center of our lives."

In his great sermon "Loving Your Enemies," Dr. King explains that Jesus's commandment of universal love with all its political implications means steadfast non-violent resistance to empire, war, and killing, and that requires total nonviolence and total surrender to the God of Universal Love: "Upheaval after upheaval has reminded us that humanity is travelling along a road called hate in a journey that will bring us to destruction and damnation. Far from being the pious injunction of a Utopian dreamer, the command to love one's enemy is an absolute necessity for our survival. Love even for enemies is the key to the solution of the problems of our world. Jesus is not an impractical idealist: he is the practical realist. . . . He realized that every genuine expression of love grows out of a consistent and total surrender to God. When he said 'Love your enemies,' he was not unmindful of its stringent qualities. Yet he meant every word of it. Our responsibility as Christians is to discover the meaning of this command and seek passionately to live it out in our daily lives."

"We still have a choice today: nonviolent coexistence or violent co-annihilation," Dr. King said at the end of his Riverside Church address on April 4, 1967. "Let us rededicate ourselves to the long and bitter—but beautiful—struggle for a new world. This is the calling of the sons and daughters of God."

༄

Not Surrendering to the False Gods of War

One hot summer afternoon Will and I went to see the movie *Oppenheimer*. The movie is about J. Robert Oppenheimer, the physicist who headed the Manhattan project, built the town of Los Alamos, and directed thousands of scientists in developing the atomic bomb and testing it on July 16, 1945, in Alamogordo, New Mexico, before it was dropped on Hiroshima and Nagasaki, killing over two hundred thousand people. I spent over fifteen years as a priest in New Mexico in the early 2000s, leading an annual public vigil for the abolition of nuclear weapons every year on the Hiroshima anniversary in Los Alamos Park in the center of town. It's now a beautiful green lawn with a pond filled with ducks and geese, but this is the exact spot where the Hiroshima bomb was physically built.

I knew the film would push my buttons. It was devastating and depressing. It showed how they built the bomb but not its effects on the people of Hiroshima and Nagasaki. When it was first dropped in the New Mexico desert, Oppenheimer quoted the Bhagavad Gita, "Now I am become death, the destroyer of worlds." In the last scene, Oppenheimer confides to Albert Einstein that they had paved the way for the destruction of the planet.

We left the theater, walked out into the hot sun, and reflected on the film. Will wanted to know how I felt about it, considering my years of outspoken resistance to the ongoing development of nuclear weapons at the Los Alamos National Labs. I said I felt no consolation from my activism against nuclear weapons, but rather, a greater sense of urgency. "We're closer to nuclear war than ever before," I said, "and I need to keep doing what

I can to build a grassroots movement of nonviolent resistance for nuclear disarmament."

Throughout the film I kept recalling the words of my friend Daniel Berrigan. The first day I met him on a retreat in the Poconos, Dan said, "What we are up against is Death with a capital 'D.' Our problem is not just violence, war, and nuclear weapons, but a global addiction to death as a social methodology." We bring good things, good people, to death, he taught. The challenge is to have nothing to do with Death, with the big business of Death, with the machinery, means and methodologies of death, whether through racism and corporate greed or militarism and weapons of mass destruction or gun violence or environmental destruction.

"Dan taught me to non-cooperate with death," I told Will. In a world addicted to death, that's the first step if we want to live in peace. "We have to stand against all the forces of death and destruction, beginning with our ongoing plans to vaporize people around the world. You and I want to non-cooperate with the forces of death and spend our lives in Universal Love serving humanity and creation. That means we'll have to stand publicly against the systems and structures of war, injustice, corporate greed, nuclear weapons, environmental destruction, and death."

If we want to deepen in the spiritual life and go all the way into full-on surrender to Universal Love and Peace, then we have to be clear about what we are *not* surrendering to, I told my friend. We choose not to surrender to the false gods of militarism, nuclear weapons, money, racism, and fossil fuels that bring billions of dollars to the super rich and their corporations but wreak havoc upon the poor and threaten creation itself.

More, as we experiment with total surrender to universal love and peace, we realize that we continue to do what we can to support the grassroots movements of nonviolent resistance to the forces of death. As I learned the hard way in New Mexico, we will be misunderstood, denounced, even threatened, but when we hold our ground, rely completely on the God of Peace, maintain our steadfast nonviolence, and pursue a vision of universal love and nonviolent conflict resolution, we will sow seeds for a future harvest of peace, whether or not we live to see it.

"Unbearable conflicts have worn us down or even made us cynical," Dietrich Bonhoeffer wrote in 1943, two years before his execution by the Nazis. "Are we still of any use? We will not need geniuses, cynics, people who have contempt for others, or cunning tacticians, but simple, uncomplicated, and honest human beings. Will our inner strength to resist what has been forced on us have remained strong enough, and our honesty with ourselves blunt enough to find our way back to simplicity and honesty?" The question hangs in the air.

"Your 'Yes' to God," Bonhoeffer concluded, "requires your 'No' to all injustice, to all evil, to all lies, to all oppression and violation of the weak and the poor." In other words, if we surrender ourselves individually and collectively to the God of Peace and Universal Love as totally as possible, there will be consequences. Doing the will of God and not our own will, means that we prepare ourselves to accept those consequences.

෴

The Political Implications of Surrendering to the God of Peace

What you soon discover, I said to Will, is that there are profound social, economic, racial, political, and environmental implications of living a life surrendered to the God of Peace and Universal Love. If we surrender ourselves to God, start living in Godly ways, doing God's will of peace, then God will live through us.

The more we let go of our personal will and endeavor to do only God's will, the more we notice how different our will is from God's will. The God of Universal Love and Peace wills that we cultivate, radiate, and practice universal love, universal compassion, universal peace, and total nonviolence toward every human being and creature on earth for the rest of our lives, and that we let God's universal love, compassion, peace, and non-violence work through us. To participate in this will of universal peace and love is to open ourselves to God's politics, to God's plans, ways, and methodologies for dealing with the whole human race and all creation. Universal love, compassion, peace, and nonviolence become a way of life, our attitude toward others, and our political stand in the world of hatred, division, and war. We no longer care about our personal wishes or the consequences of such a political stand for ourselves. We have surrendered to the God of Universal Love and Peace, so if people denounce us, reject us, and dismiss us because of our universal loving approach to life, we respond peacefully, prayerfully, mindfully, and lovingly, and continue to surrender it all to God and to pray for everyone, beginning with those who reject us.

Thomas Merton lived as a Trappist monk in silence and communal prayer, and eventually retreated to a hermitage in the woods to surrender himself completely to God alone, yet his monastic life had specific political consequences, he realized. In 1956, he wrote that this life of "humility and silence" in a world of violence and war "was itself a statement." And in 1966 he explained his life of prayer, solitude, and peace in the Preface to the Japanese edition of *The Seven Storey Mountain* this way:

It is my intention to make my entire life a rejection of, a protest against the crimes and injustices of war and political tyranny which threaten to destroy the whole human race and the world. By my monastic life and vows, I am saying no to all the concentration camps, the aerial bombardments, the staged political trials, the judicial murders, the racial injustices, the economic tyrannies, and the whole socio-economic apparatus which seems geared for nothing but global destruction in spite of all its fair words in favor of peace. I make my monastic silence a protest against the lies of politicians, propagandists, and agitators, and when I speak it is to deny that my faith and my Church can ever seriously be aligned with these forces of injustice and destruction. My life must, then, be a protest against those also, and perhaps against those most of all. . . . If I say NO to all these secular forces, I also say YES to all that is good in the world and in man. I say yes to all that is beautiful in nature. . . . I say yes to all the men and women who are my brothers and sisters in the world.

This great teacher of peace, compassion, prayer, universal love, and nonviolence invites us to consider our surrender to the God of Peace as a lifelong peaceful protest against war, poverty, greed, racism, gun violence, executions, nuclear weapons, and environmental destruction. As we say no to the culture of violence, racism, and war, we also say yes to all that is good in the world and in humanity, to all the nonviolent movements for justice, disarmament, and creation, to all the beauty in the world and in humanity. Though alone and in solitude, Merton inspired many to take up the challenge of living nonviolently, surrendered to the God of Peace. With his steadfast, faithful example, we too can surrender ourselves to God, take our antiwar stand in the world, and let the chips fall where they may. Perhaps like Merton, we will inspire others to walk in the way of peace.

∽

Getting with the Program:
Joining the Global Grassroots Movement
of Nonviolence

"Isn't surrendering to Universal Love giving up and becoming completely passive?" Will asked the other day. He said he had given it much thought and was beginning to think that this was a life of complete passivity.

"On the contrary," I answered, "if we sincerely surrender ourselves repeatedly for the rest of our lives to Universal Love, to the God of Peace and Nonviolence, in response to the reality of our selfishness and violence, and the world's violence, instead of being passive, we become more active than ever. We become public activists, jump into the fray, and do what we think Universal Love, the God of Peace, wants us to do. As extensions of Universal Love, we get involved with suffering humanity and creation. Love is not passive; love is always active. It reaches out to include, welcome, reconcile, disarm, heal, bless, and embrace every human being, every creature, and all creation so that all might dwell in God's peace."

It's hard to believe that any of us can make a difference in such a world, but as extensions of Universal Love, I suggested, we don't even think like that. We go forward anyway, do what we can, and let God make a difference through us. We do what we can to spread universal love and its social, racial, economic, political, and environmental implications. If we each pitch in, pick a cause, and contribute once, twice, or three times a day for the struggle for justice, disarmament, and creation, as God leads us, and never give up, God can use us through waves of love to inspire and create justice and peace.

Historian Howard Zinn insisted that the crucial difference in every historically successful grassroots movement was the steadfast commitment of ordinary people who did something each day for the movement—even if they knew they themselves would not live to see the transformation they sought. When the commitment is total, the outcome is assured. Why? Because nonviolence is contagious. Eventually, people will be won over through nonviolent suffering love, truth, and wisdom. Remember Gandhi's dictum, I told Will: "Full effort is full victory."

"To be hopeful in hard times is based on the fact that human history is not only a story of cruelty, but also of compassion, sacrifice, courage and kindness," Zinn wrote in "The Optimism of Uncertainty," in 2004. "If we see only the worst, it destroys our capacity to do something. If we remember those times and places where people have behaved magnificently, this gives us the energy to act. And if we do act, in however small a way, we do not have to wait for some grand utopian future. The future is an infinite succession of presents and to live now as we think human beings should live, in defiance of all that is bad around us, is itself a marvelous victory."

Historically, great positive social change happens through people power, grassroots movements of nonviolence. From the abolitionists and the suffragists, to the labor movement of the 1930s to the civil rights movement of the 1950s and 1960s, to the antiwar, environmental, and women's movements of the 1970s, to the thousands of movements that are sweeping over the world today, ordinary people have organized and mobilized to wield the power of nonviolence and break down the most intransigent unjust structures. We can ponder the peaceful resistance that led to the end of segregation in the South, the Berlin Wall, Communism, Apartheid, the Marcos dictatorship, and the Liberian dictatorship. These nonviolent transformations happened because people took to the streets in active, public, nonviolent resistance to demand change, and they never backed down. They did not give up, nor did they strike out. They simply stood their ground in a spirit of universal love and truth until the victory of justice.

The life of surrender to God, I think, pushes us into the thick of things more than we might have thought possible. We end up joining the struggles and movements for positive social change, every day using the tools of nonviolence so that we act with grace, love, and kindness toward ourselves and one another, and then try in humility and patience to inspire social, racial, and economic justice, global disarmament, and environmental sustainability. As we recognize the enormity of the task at hand, we realize we do not have time for despair, apathy, fear, or worry. We keep surrendering to God, allowing ourselves to be transformed into extensions of Universal Love and becoming channels of peace in our war-making world. If we let the God of Peace and Universal Love lead us, use us, and work through us, then we will have done our part to help disarm our world. The more we surrender ourselves to the God of Peace and God's work of peace in a world of war, the more we will become change agents of universal love. Together, we can become tipping-point people like Rosa Parks who make a difference and spark social change.

But as Mother Teresa once said, we have to give God permission. We have to surrender ourselves to God and say, "Yes, God, I give you permission to use me however you want for your will, your work, your plan of love for humanity."

༄

Philip Berrigan's Surrendered Life of Nonviolent Resistance

One of the most powerful tipping-point persons I have known was Philip Berrigan, Dan's younger brother and cohort in the work of peace and disarmament. Throughout his long life Phil served as a catalyst who brought people into the civil rights, peace, and antinuclear movements, right up until his death in 2002. In 2024, my friend Brad Wolf published *A Ministry of Risk*, the first collection of Phil's writings, mainly from jails and prisons. His life of surrender to the God of Peace led to lifelong nonviolent resistance to the culture of war and death in ways perhaps unmatched by few others in US history.

Daniel and Philip Berrigan were legendary figures in the 1960s, 1970s, and 1980s, household names for their

arrest and imprisonment for burning draft files in the
Catonsville Nine action against the Vietnam War. Later
they took part in the first Plowshares disarmament ac-
tion, hammering on missile warheads in reenactment of
Isaiah's prophecy of hammering swords into plowshares.
For me, they were mentors, jail mates, and friends.

I met Phil in 1982, when I was twenty-two years
old, during a Christmas retreat in a church basement
in Washington, DC, which ended with nonviolent civil
disobedience at the Pentagon to mark the Feast of the
Holy Innocents. Meeting Phil was like meeting Ezekiel,
Jonah, or Jeremiah himself. I'd never met anyone like
him. He was like the great abolitionists of the nine-
teenth century, like William Lloyd Garrison, Frederick
Douglass, or even John Brown. He spoke the truth
fiercely, talked about nuclear disarmament passionately,
and urged everyone he met to engage in nonviolent civil
disobedience and resistance to the culture of war. He
had the greatest sense of urgency of anyone I've ever
met. During the twenty years I knew him, he was always in jail, in court, awaiting sentencing, or planning
his next action.

If you were with him, you had to get involved in
the peace movement. You could not remain neutral in
his presence. He told everyone he met to get involved,
come to the next protest, speak out, and risk arrest in
resistance to the culture of war. It was just a matter of

months after meeting him that I was first arrested for a protest at the Pentagon.

Through his and Dan's example, I learned to make nonviolent resistance to the culture of violence a way of life, a regular part of my faith in action. I cannot remember all the talks, protests, and arrests with them in the 1980s because there were so many. As of this writing, I've been arrested eighty-five times, but each of them was arrested hundreds of times for their public stand against war and injustice. It was indeed a way of life, but more important, a way of discipleship to the nonviolent Jesus, a way of living out their total surrender to the God of Peace. It was an expression of faith, enacted in love, compassion, truth, and nonviolence, which targeted the structures of mass murder. They were living extensions of Universal Love.

I corresponded with or saw Phil regularly until the night of his death. I heard him speak many times, and I had begun to speak out for justice and peace myself when I finally felt moved to join them in a Plowshares disarmament action—what became the Pax Christi-Spirit of Life Plowshares action in 1993.

With our dear friends Bruce Friedrich and Lynn Fredriksson, Phil and I walked onto the Seymour Johnson Air Force Base in Goldsboro, North Carolina, right through national wargames, approached an F-15e nuclear-capable fighter bomber on alert to bomb the former

Yugoslavia, and hammered several times on it to fulfill Isaiah's mandate "to beat swords into plowshares." We each faced twenty years in prison. Phil and I landed in a tiny jail cell for eight months in rural North Carolina, with young Bruce in the next cell over, and we never left our cells except once or twice for the entire time.

It was the most intense, difficult, and blessed experience of my life. Phil was in the bottom bunk, I was in the top bunk, there was an open toilet, and the space was about ten feet by ten feet. Bruce was allowed to come into our cell, courtesy of the warden whom we befriended, and together we embarked on a sort of modern-day "monastic routine." Lights came on at 6 a.m., they gave us black water (which they called coffee) and usually a slice of bread and something that resembled beans, then we held a quick check-in to see how we each were feeling. Then we embarked on a two-hour gospel study. As we read through Mark and John over those long months, I learned more about Jesus in that jail cell than in four years of graduate theology school. This was followed by the breaking of the bread and passing of the cup (in this case, stale grape juice that we received once a week in a little plastic container). Then we tackled the mail. Phil and I each received about fifty letters a day. After a quick lunch, we spent twenty minutes together in prayer, mainly petitioning the God of Peace for the gifts of peace. Then, we began a one-hour period of timed, disciplined writing. Over many months we churned out dozens of articles and essays for journals around the world.

So many moments stand out. On Christmas 1993 we had nothing to do, so I asked Phil to tell us the story of his life. He talked for a week, with Bruce and me literally sitting at his feet, taking in all the details. I'm not sure he had ever told anyone his life story like that—who gets to experience that?—but we were overwhelmed and inspired. It was like sitting at the feet of St. Peter or St. Paul. Afterward, I suggested he put it all on paper, and a year after he was released, he published his auto-biography, *Fighting the Lamb's War*.

We endured many arraignments, being led around in chains, meeting all kinds of visitors, being interviewed by the press, dealing with the guards, wardens, prosecu-tors, FBI agents, judges, and marshals. Eventually we were released, and as I recall, about a year later, he was back in prison and I was visiting him. I shared one year of his lifelong resistance, and I'm still trying to process it. I cannot imagine what it felt like to live his life, to be Philip Berrigan.

Altogether, Phil spent over eleven years of his life in prison for taking public nonviolent action in Jesus's name against war and nuclear weapons. Resistance to the culture of war was his ordinary day-to-day way of living. I attended many of his trials but was usually not allowed to visit him because of my own criminal record.

In the spring of 2002, Phil was released from prison after several years for his last Plowshares action. I met him that May at a massive antiwar demonstration at the Washington monument. He was frail, using a cane, suffering from hip pain, but as feisty as ever. He then underwent hip surgery and never recovered. On the morning of October 5, I called him for his birthday, and he told me that he just walked in the door after getting the bad news from the doctor that cancer had spread all through him and he had only a short time to live.

In early December 2002, several of us journeyed to Jonah House in Baltimore to join his family—Liz, Frida, Jerry and Katie, and brothers Dan and Jerry—in vigil. He died on a cold Friday night with dozens of family and friends with him. It was one of the most powerful experiences of community and care for the dying that any of us, including Liz and Dan, had ever experienced. I presided at his funeral a few days later in a packed inner-city church. A small circle of family and friends buried him later that night at the nearby cemetery. We stood under massive, fiery torches, lowered him into the ground, poured holy water on the coffin, and offered prayers, blessings, and gratitude. One friend said it felt like a scene out of *Lord of the Rings*, like the burial of King Arthur or one of the knights of the Roundtable. We were burying one of the greatest prophets of peace in modern history, and we knew it. Really, we were celebrating his resurrection into the eternal life of peace and pledging to carry on his steadfast determination to do what we could to end war, nuclear weapons, and injustice, and welcome God's reign of justice and nonviolence here on earth. In our hearts we tasted the fullness of peace he must now experience as a consequence of his fully surrendered life.

During the march to the church for Phil's funeral, I overheard our friend, actor Martin Sheen, telling Amy Goodman of "Democracy Now" what he had learned from Phil. "Phil took the Gospel personally," Martin said. I was stunned by that insight. Phil acted upon every word of Jesus as if it was directed to him personally. That is what every Christian is supposed to do, I thought, but do I really do it?

I remember one moment long ago in that dungeon-like North Carolina jail cell. It was late morning, and we were reading the pile of letters that had just been delivered. Thousands were writing to support us and encourage us, and many of them said the same thing: "I wish I had your courage." Phil was reading one such letter, when he put it down, and said to me with a bit of frustration, "Can you believe these people? Saying they wish they had our courage?"

I was a young, clueless whippersnapper, so of course I had no idea what he was talking about. I was sitting in jail with the great Phil Berrigan, facing twenty years in prison, and I wished I had his courage! To hide my own ignorance, I said, "No, I can't believe they would say that. Tell me more." With that he said, "They don't seem to realize—it's not about courage. It's about faith."

Suddenly, I understood Phil and Dan in a deeper way. Everything they did flowed from their profound faith in the God of Peace and Love, which required of them total surrender. They were not so much courageous activists, as faith-filled, surrendered disciples of the nonviolent Jesus and keepers and doers of the word of God. While millions claim to be fundamentalist Christians who study the word of God, Phil let the word of God form and change him. He took the fundamental bottom line teachings of the Gospels as matters of life and death, as they are, and so he put those commandments first and foremost in everything he did: "Love your enemies, hunger and thirst for justice, be as compassionate as God, put down the sword, offer no violent resistance to one who does evil, and seek first God's reign and God's justice." He lived according to these hard gospel teachings and became a true disciple of the nonviolent Jesus and thus a prophet of peace to the world of war, which is the mark of authentic biblical faith and witness.

Phil also insisted that resistance must become the new normal, ordinary way of life in this culture of war and death. From now on, we live as Phil and Dan did in permanent nonviolent resistance to war-making and every form of violence and injustice. We do not have to spend eleven years of our lives in prison, like Phil, but we have to do something to contribute to the bottom up, people-power grassroots movement of nonviolent resistance and positive social change, they demanded. Phil wrote the following from Danbury Federal Correctional Institution in 1971: "Common sense tells me that the profession of life requires an unalterable resistance to the high and mighty, who pose as patrons of humanity while they destroy humanity. Resistance is essential. Without it, one cannot realize humanity in oneself or in others, only illusion, comfort, and escape."

Unlike most Christians, Phil spoke regularly about taking up the cross. Who talks about that anymore? Even in church we rarely hear sermons encouraging us to take up the cross and follow the nonviolent Jesus in public opposition to systemic injustice, war, and empire. The cross has been watered down into any personal, private difficulty. We get a flat tire, and we tell ourselves we're carrying our cross. "War, racism, and poverty can be traced to our desire to avoid the cross," Phil wrote. He understood that the cross was capital punishment for the capital crime of nonviolent resistance against systemic injustice and empire. When the gospel of Jesus calls us to take up the cross, it summons us to carry on Jesus's grassroots campaign of permanent nonviolent resistance to the culture of violence and war, even unto suffering and death—and to accept the political consequences.

That's what total surrender to God looked like for Philip Berrigan.

For Phil, the work of peace and disarmament was costly and a requirement of faith in the God of Peace. If we were not causing "good trouble," if the war-making government was not threatened by our efforts to make peace, he argued, then we were not following Jesus, taking up the cross, or surrendering ourselves to God's will.

Phil Berrigan's life, writings, and witness from prison for his antiwar action pose radical questions for every one of us. In this world of perpetual war, nuclear weapons, systemic injustice, racism, poverty, and environmental destruction, he asks: What are we going to do about the global crisis we find ourselves in? Are we going to stand on the sidelines and do nothing? Are we going to enjoy the benefits of the culture of violence and war, and live comfortably while billions suffer and die? Or dare we join Jesus's grassroots campaign of revolutionary nonviolence, resist the war machine, non-cooperate with the culture of violence, and speak out for the coming of God's reign of peace on earth? What does the God of Peace require of us? In one of his essays from jail, "Isaiah in North Carolina," Phil writes: "A simple choice beckons: Are we going to be people of perpetual war with darkened souls and bloody hands? Or are we going to dare to be the sons and daughters of our nonviolent, just, and compassionate God, who face the world's lunacy disarmed?"

In "Truth and Peace Mean Resistance," written from prison to his supporters, he encourages them with these words: "Let's build a real movement by building real people. Let's give one another hope and love. That's what people need—hope and love. Let's push back the darkness! That's what they said about Jesus—he pushed back the darkness once and for all!"

✎

Fire Drill Fridays

A few years ago the Swedish teenager Greta Thunberg stood before the United Nations and declared that the world house is on fire, and we need to start acting accordingly. Her message, while praised by some, was ignored by Western politicians. Over the years she has continued to speak out and call for action and to inspire a whole new generation of young people to take a stand.

In a 2019 address to the British Parliament she said: "The climate crisis is both the easiest and the hardest issue we have ever faced. The easiest because we know what we must do. We must stop the emissions of greenhouse gases. The hardest because our current economics are still totally dependent on burning fossil fuels, and thereby destroying ecosystems to create everlasting economic growth. . . . So, we can't save the world by playing by the rules, because the rules have to be changed. Everything needs to change and it has to start today.

And she told the audience at the 2019 World Economic Forum in Davos: "Adults keep saying: 'We owe it to the young people to give them hope.' But I don't want your hope, I don't want you to be hopeful. I want you to panic. I want you to feel the fear I feel every day. And then I want you to act. I want you to act as you would in a crisis. I want you to act as if the house is on fire. Because it is."

At the Pre-COP26 Youth4Climate conference in Milan in 2021 she famously said, "We can no longer let the people in power decide what is politically possible. We can no longer let the people in power decide what hope is. Hope is not passive. Hope is not blah, blah, blah. Hope is telling the truth. Hope is taking action. And hope always comes from the people."

In a 2019 conversation with Alexandria Ocasio-Cortez, Thunberg said, "I know so many people who feel hopeless, and they ask me, 'What should I do?' And I say: 'Act. Do something.' Because that is the best medicine against sadness and depression."

Inspired by Greta's urgent calls, longtime actor and activist Jane Fonda decided she had to do something. In her eighties, she moved from Beverly Hills to

Washington, DC, where, with the help of Greenpeace, she launched Fire Drill Fridays, a grassroots campaign of weekly civil disobedience at the US Capitol to mobilize people and enact legislation to stop environmental destruction.

Her movement took off. Every Friday in the fall of 2019, more than a thousand people gathered on the lawn of the US Capitol to rally and call for legislation to end the use of fossil fuels, and then to engage in "nonviolent direct action" to push Congress.

As I followed these developments, prayed over Greta's and Jane's public stand, and tried to surrender my life to God the Creator, I felt moved to join the campaign. So, one cold December morning, a few months before the pandemic broke, I journeyed to DC and joined over a thousand people on the lawn in front of the US Capitol. We heard powerful speeches from leaders such as civil rights icon Dolores Huerta, Women's Rights advocate Gloria Steinem, Buddhist leader Roshi Joan Halifax, Poor Peoples' Campaign leader Rev. William Barber II, and Jane herself, who called for an army of people to take to the streets for climate justice. We chanted slogans ("Tell me what democracy looks like? This is what democracy looks like!" "What do we want? Climate Justice! When do we want it? Now!"). We sang ("This Little Light of Mine," "Ain't Gonna Let Nobody Turn Me Around"). We held banners

("We want a Green New Deal now!"). Our message to the US Senate was Greta's: "The eyes of all future generations are upon you. We will not let you get away with this. The world is waking up. And whether you like it or not, change is coming!"

Then we walked a few blocks to the Hart Senate Office Building, and in an act of nonviolent civil disobedience, 138 of us gathered in the rotunda and started singing as we held our signs. The building was shut down, and one by one we were handcuffed, booked, and photographed, then loaded into paddy wagons and hauled off to an old police warehouse in Southwest DC. There we sat in our handcuffs for the rest of the day, the men on one side, the women on the other, greeting each other, sharing our experiences, and waiting our turn to be interviewed and eventually released, most of us late in the evening.

You could say it did no good. You could dismiss the whole thing cynically as an exercise in vainglory, ego run amok, naiveté, or even recklessness. You could even confess functional despair and say it's all too late, nothing can be done—but then you would be doing exactly what the oil companies and their politicians want. But I kept thinking, this *is* what democracy looks like. More, this is the political consequence of surrendering our lives completely to the Creator as greedy corporations and nations destroy the planet. This is the power of bottom-up, people-power, grassroots movements of creative nonviolence, and the witness of front-line people who break bad laws that legalize death and destruction and accept the consequences. In this case, we were disturbing the peace on behalf of Mother Earth, trying to break through "business as usual" and demand action to stop the world from burning down.

It felt empowering to stand up, or in this case, to sit down on behalf of Mother Earth at the seat of global power, and to discover we have more power as ordinary people than we realize. Dr. King was right—creative active nonviolence is power. Given the horror of catastrophic climate change, however, I think we need to go way beyond Gandhi and Dr. King and build a global, grassroots, people-power movement of active nonviolence on behalf of all creation the likes of which the world has never seen. The regular, repeated, steadfast, serious yet joyful nonviolent rallies, marches, and civil disobedience in Washington, DC, point a way to the ongoing nonviolent resistance that is needed if we are to spark a social transformation for a more just, peaceful, and environmentally sustainable future.

For me, however, that Fire Drill Friday brought an unexpected gift: it was a profound spiritual experience. That whole day unleashed for me and my friends an inner joy that I had not known in a long time. I dare say, most everyone felt the same thing. During the long, cold hours when we sat handcuffed in that police warehouse, everyone smiled, chatted, and sang, and an instant community was formed around our action. We had all stepped away from the normalcy of our lives and literally crossed a line into the unknown. What we encountered, instead of fear, was joy—the joy over taking public action, the joy of speaking out together, the joy of choosing hope over despair, and the joy of surrendering together to the God of Peace.

I'll never forget that day. It showed me the power of collective surrender to Universal Love and Peace, of welcoming the political implications of our public stand on behalf of creation and our inner stand on behalf of the Creator—and the communal consequence and experience of joy that come with it.

∻

"You Want Me to Get Rid of My Guns?"

Once, I led a day-long retreat entitled "Jesus, St. Francis, and Gospel Nonviolence" to a packed church at the Franciscan Renewal Center in Scottsdale. I pointed out the peacemaking practices and teachings of Jesus and Francis and suggested some steps we could take to be more nonviolent like them, and to work for a more nonviolent Phoenix, a more nonviolent Arizona, and a more nonviolent world. We ended with a beautiful mass for peace and a commissioning service to go forth and make peace.

Afterward, at 5 p.m., a gentleman approached me and asked point blank: "Are you actually saying that you are against war and violence?"

I was stunned, because in fact I had been pleading my case since 9 a.m. that morning that war and violence do not work, that peace and nonviolence were our future, and that living peace and nonviolence was the will of God and the path to God.

"But are you saying that Jesus and St. Francis were nonviolent and would want me to be nonviolent? Does that mean you want me to get rid of my guns?"

I looked at him quizzically. "Yes," I said calmly.

"I have hundreds of guns in my house," he said. "But if you tell me, I will get rid of them."

"Yes," I said with a smile. "I invite you, in the name of Jesus and St. Francis, to go home and get rid of all your guns and weapons and start a new journey of gospel nonviolence."

"Okay," he said, and walked away.

The following week he emailed me. "With the help of family and friends, I dug a big hole in my backyard, buried all my guns, poured concrete on them, and buried them with dirt."

I was astonished and thanked him profusely. "Praise God," I said.

His action gave me hope and encouragement to keep trying publicly to help others disarm, just as I continue to try to surrender myself to God and let God disarm my heart repeatedly. Perhaps we can all help one another to disarm—and I mean, first, literally disarm—as a step forward in discipleship to the nonviolent Jesus and surrender to the God of Peace.

I often remind myself that during the first few months of the Montgomery Bus Boycott in late 1955 and early 1956, the young Rev. Martin Luther King, Jr., slept with a gun under his pillow, even while giving brilliant speeches calling for nonviolence. When my friend Glenn Smiley and Bayard Rustin from the Fellowship of Reconciliation journeyed from New York to Montgomery to advise him on the tactics and strategies of nonviolence, and learned of his gun, they told him that he could not call others to be nonviolent and trust in God if he himself wasn't doing that. It may seem obvious now, but Dr. King had to learn the implications of surrender and nonviolence just like the rest of us—slowly, painstakingly, one step at a time. He too had to get rid of his guns, and he had to stop allowing armed men to protect him, and in doing so, he became a more authentic, more powerful, and fearless witness of nonviolence. He had to learn repeatedly like the rest of us to surrender himself to God, to trust in God, and to live in God's way of total nonviolence, even in an atmosphere of fear, racism, and violence. For King, that meant handing over his life, his security, and every outcome to God. It means the same for us.

In 2024, the surgeon general declared gun violence a national public health crisis. These days, we face a real political crisis because we are all being held hostage by NRA gun extremists. But as I ponder it, I realize we're dealing with something deeper: a spiritual crisis.

We're told guns make us safer, but if that were true, we'd be the safest country in the world. Reputable internet sources like Pew Research Organization, report that there are more guns in the United States than people, perhaps four hundred million guns in circulation. In the last decade over one million people have been shot to death in the United States; 1.5 million since 1968, more than all Americans killed in our wars. Shooting deaths in the United States are twenty-five times higher than in other countries. The suicide rate in the United States is ten times higher than in most other countries. In 2022, 48,111 people died in gun violence; that is, 27,000 people shot themselves, and 20,000 were shot by others; 1 death every 11 minutes. As I write this, every day 327 people are shot in the United States , and on average 117 will die. Moreover, 42 percent of those who own and use guns claim to be Christians.

Mass shootings only make up 1 percent of all US gun violence. In 2023, there were 656 mass shootings.

In 2021, there were 690. We grieve for the dead and wounded in Sandy Hook, Connecticut; the Parkland, Florida, high school; Virginia tech; the Charleston, South Carolina, AME Church; the Aurora, Colorado, movie theater; the Orlando Pulse Dance Club; the Las Vegas concert where over 850 people were shot, the Pittsburgh synagogue; and many more places. Since 1997, there have been over fifteen hundred school shootings.

I have traveled in numerous warzones and known many people who were later shot and killed, and I have received many death threats—including from some of my own New Mexico parishioners for speaking out against the Iraq War and Los Alamos. I always remember the six Jesuit priests of El Salvador, where I lived and worked in 1985, who were later assassinated in 1989.

In 2012, I went to Afghanistan and listened for several long days to dozens of young people telling us how their families were killed by US drones. I flew from Albuquerque to Kabul, and it was a long trip, so I decided to stop along the way and visit my older brother. He and his family lived in a little village in Connecticut that no one ever heard of called Sandy Hook. He was furious at me for going to Afghanistan and taking such risks for peace, and he said no one could make a difference anyway. He was the editor of the Danbury newspaper, and I told him he should be doing more to end the violence in Connecticut. It was a tense visit, after which I drove from Sandy Hook to JFK Airport on Long Island and flew to Kabul, Afghanistan. I caught pneumonia while I was there and flew home to see my parents in DC, but first went straight to the hospital. Then I drove to New York City to speak on "Democracy Now" about my trip. It was Friday morning, December 14, 2012, that, sick and exhausted, I told Amy Goodman about Kabul and the stories of the young people whose relatives were killed by our drone attacks. That same day the shooter walked into the Sandy Hook elementary school and shot and killed twenty-six kids and teachers. My brother lived two houses down from the school. They were put under lockdown all that day. Ever since, Sandy Hook and Afghanistan and Los Alamos are forever linked in my mind. For me, it is all one global system of violence, a global addiction to violence, a global illness that plagues us all.

When Daniel Berrigan visited El Salvador and Nicaragua in 1984 during the US wars, he concluded that perhaps the best we could work for is a world of "gunlessness." I've spent my life wondering about these things and trying to pursue those visions of peace. That led me in the 2010s, to go with a group of friends to the Round House in Santa Fe, the New Mexico state capital, to speak at an open hearing calling for background checks for people who buy guns at the massive gun shows along the Mexican border, where a person can walk in, buy an automatic assault weapon, and walk out, no questions asked.

The room was packed with NRA members. Most NRA members support background checks, but there is a well-organized minority of gun extremists. As I listened to them that day, I was amazed at their anger and their commitment to guns at any price, and I kept wondering why. It seemed to me that they felt empowered by their guns, by the belief that guns gave them security and protected them, and that guns, ultimately, gave them their identity. When I consider the calling to surrender our lives to God, I notice the various other things we surrender ourselves to. In this case I left thinking that we have to help one another find our true identity not in guns, not in our bombs, not in the flag, not in America, but in the living God of Peace. This is the basis of gospel nonviolence and faith in God. Anything else is idolatry.

The Gospel of Luke tells the story of Jesus being baptized in the Jordan River, then sitting down in prayer when the Holy Spirit came upon him and a voice said, "You are my beloved." I think from that moment on, Jesus knew who he was. He claimed this word as his true identity. He always would be the beloved of God, regardless the circumstances. When he walked into the desert to pray and meditate over this powerful realization, of course, he was tempted to reject this identity. That's the spiritual life in a nutshell. To claim our identities as the beloved sons and daughters of the God of Peace means surrendering our lives to the God of Peace and fulfilling our identity.

The tempting inner voices of doubt, despair, and domination that challenged Jesus said, "Oh, yeah? You think you are the beloved son of God? If you are the son of God, prove it." He rejected those temptations as the seeds of violence, as the voices that feed our inner addiction to violence. Instead, he claimed his true identity as the son of the God of Peace, which meant he would live in total nonviolence and radiate the peace of God.

What continues to amaze me is that in his Sermon on the Mount, Jesus announces that we are all invited to be the blessed sons and daughters of God! He tells us who we are and invites us to claim our true identities, to discover the fullness of our identity in the living God of Peace. "Blessed are the peacemakers," he teaches. "They shall be called the sons and daughters of God" (Matt 5:9). In other words, "You are all the beloved sons and daughters of the God of Peace."

I remember reading this verse forty years ago during the thirty-day silent retreat of St. Ignatius, the *Spiritual Exercises,* and realizing, "Oh, so that's who I am, that's my real identity, that's who I'm called to be: not a son of a gun, the son of the Bomb, the son of the US military, the son of America or a political party or Wall Street or the US flag or the NRA or Los Alamos, but a son of the living

God of Peace. Like every other human being, I'm invited to live as a peacemaker, as a child of the God of Peace."

Most of my life's work since then has been trying to live out this truth and inviting others to discover it for themselves. As I look back, I see the many times and places where I did not trust in the God of Peace and fell into the many traps of violence—all because I had yet to learn the wisdom of total surrender to God, to let go of all control of my life, ultimately to let go of my ego and give every moment to God and enter the liminal space of God's peace and universal love.

My friend Charlie McCarthy first defined nonviolence as remembering who we are. Violence, he said, comes from forgetting who we are. Perhaps the best service we can offer to one another, then, is to help all people claim their true identities as beloved sons and daughters of the God of Peace so they no longer look for meaning in guns, weapons, money, and war, and instead become their best selves dwelling in peace with God and creation. If we are sons and daughters of God, then every human being is our sister and brother, and we can never hurt or kill anyone. Given the state of our country and our world, that means that when the occasion arises, we can dare invite one another to get rid of our guns, quit the military, stop profiting from war and weapons, and begin the journey of surrender. As I have tried to do this,

I have found it to be an exciting and fulfilling challenge, and I hope others will take up the challenge, too.

∾

Abolishing the Death Penalty

Daniel Berrigan wrote that after Vietnam, nonviolent resistance had to become a permanent way of life. In his book *The Dark Night of Resistance*, written while he was underground and being hunted by the FBI, he proposed what he called "the state of resistance as a state of life itself. Like it or not, this is the shape of things," he wrote. "We will not again know sweet normalcy in our lifetime."

If our surrender to the God of Peace requires resistance to the systems of violence and death that run the world and tear us apart, then some of us, like Dorothy Day and Daniel Berrigan, have to make a public show of it to break through the complicity, silence, and apathy of the times. There are many ways to do this, and many instances in which we can respond. In the end, I find, it comes down to a matter of discernment, of feeling our way through life and letting the Holy Spirit lead us, sometimes "where we would rather not go" as the risen Jesus tells Peter (Jn 21).

One such instance came for me when my buddy Shane Claiborne called and invited me to join him and his friends in a public witness at the US Supreme Court. "It's the fortieth anniversary of the modern death penalty," he said, "and we've decided to do something to mark the occasion, and I really want you to come with me." I prayed over it, sensed the beckoning finger of God, and so I went.

It was a cold and rainy January morning that day as eighteen of us church folk and anti–death penalty activists, climbed the massive white steps of the Supreme Court and unfurled an enormous banner, the size of a billboard, which read "Stop Executions!" We sang songs, offered prayers, and dropped red roses on the ground to commemorate the 1,442 people killed by the state over the previous forty years. Nearly three thousand prisoners are currently on death rows in thirty-one states. I have met over two dozen who were eventually killed, and I have advocated for an end to the death penalty all my life. But some of our group included members of Murder Victims' Families for Reconciliation. These good people lost immediate family members who were killed by people now on death row for their crimes, and yet they stood publicly against the death penalty and wanted their relatives' murderers to be given life in prison instead. Others included leaders and ministers from Black Lives Matter, Sojourners, and Red Letter Christians.

At the center of our group was Derrick Jamison, one of the sweetest and bravest persons I have ever met, who spent twenty years on death row for a crime he did not commit. A tall, gentle person, he came close to being executed six times but was eventually released when DNA evidence proved that he was innocent and that someone else committed the crime.

Hundreds of supporters watched and sang as the police began to arrest us one by one. I watched Derrick with awe and wonder as he was led away in handcuffs—back into prison for saying no to the death penalty. After all he had been through, he was willing to take a risk and suffer again so that others might live.

The action was beautiful, but it was not easy. The police put the cuffs on as tight as possible, and we heard the commander say, "Put them through the system." The officer who arrested me pulled my right hand back hard and deliberately pinched the nerve on my thumb. I was sure he was going to break my hand. One minister friend cried out so loudly we thought that his officer did break both his hand and shoulder. He was taken away in an ambulance. We were chained by the ankles, waists, and behind our backs, and it was very painful. We then spent two horrific days in chains and jail. We were only given a little water twice, and two pieces of bread with something on it they called baloney. I gladly gave mine away.

After twelve hours we were brought to the DC Central Cellblock, a place I have known well since the early 1980s. We were divided into pairs and put into tiny cells with steel bunks to lie on and bright fluorescent lights above us. My friend Doug was with me. I climbed up onto the top metal bunk, hoping to fall asleep, and was immediately surrounded by hundreds of cockroaches. It was a scene out of *Indiana Jones*. My friend Art Laffin yelled from another cell, "If you don't touch them or attack them, they won't climb on to you." That was cold comfort. We did not touch the cockroaches, but a hundred of them clung to the wall one foot from my face. Meanwhile, the fluorescent light was about two feet above me.

Not one person in our group slept that night, and we each went through our own terrible ordeal. Several felt nauseated the entire time. I was considered an old-timer, since I am an ex-con. I should have been ready for that, and I thought, of course, that I was. But I wasn't.

About 2 a.m., what with my exhaustion, the bright lights, my hunger, the cockroaches, and the unknown future, I went into a full-blown panic attack. I had trouble breathing, became incredibly anxious, and suddenly felt terrified. I sat up, called down to Doug, and said I was in trouble and needed his help immediately. I told him what was happening. We said a prayer, and I asked him to start talking in order to take my mind off all these concerns. Earlier, he mentioned that he was a Bruce Springsteen fan, and while I love Bruce's music, I told him I was a Beatles fanatic. Let's argue about Bruce, I suggested. He was game, and so we talked and argued for the next four hours about the wonders of Bruce Springsteen. Slowly, I calmed down, began to breathe easy, and regained my composure. I'm eternally grateful to God, Doug, and Bruce Springsteen for that. And the Beatles.

Late the next day our group was taken out of our cells, lined up against a wall, and chained together. We had chains around our ankles, wrists, and waists with which we were then chained to one another. We were led slowly to a main waiting cell that was crowded with hundreds of other guys who had also been arrested the previous day. Our chains were removed, but we were so crowded we could not sit or lie down, only stand shoulder to shoulder next to each other for the entire day. What I remember most of that God-awful day was that it took me a full hour to get a guard's attention to be led down the hallway to use the bathroom while he watched, with his gun ready, in case I made a break for it.

Around 4 p.m., I was called to a glass window and found my friend Mark Goldstone, one of our pro-bono lawyers, who had come to the rescue. He announced that we would be arraigned that evening. I had spent the day listening to my comrades and their life stories, but Mark was a breath of fresh air. He had helped me on perhaps twenty other occasions when I found myself behind bars for some troublemaking gospel-making research. He recommended that I plead guilty and brace myself for sixty days in prison plus a five thousand dollar fine. This made me laugh, but I had the longest criminal record of anyone in our group. The government was clearly going after us. Eventually, late that night, we were brought into court, where most of us pled guilty and were given a trial date later in the year. I was eventually given time served.

Ours was the largest act of nonviolent civil disobedience against the death penalty in US history. But what good did it do? everyone asked me. I answered the best way I could, the only way I know: positive social change comes through grassroots movements, as Jesus, Gandhi, and King showed, and sooner or later, we each have to get with the program, stand up, speak out, cross a line, and pay the price if we want a more nonviolent world. Peacemaking is costly, and as Dan Berrigan always told me, we have to pay up. What I've learned since then, however, is that such actions test my surrender to God and deepen my faith, hope, and trust in God in ways I could never expect or explain. Despite it all, my friends and I felt empowered, filled with hope, and ready for seconds! We felt we were aligned with the nonviolent Jesus, who was executed by the empire for his nonviolent resistance, and we experienced the consolation of surrender to the living God of Peace. Indeed, we felt, I dare say, like extensions of Universal Love.

"What do you think of that, Will?" I would ask after telling stories like this.

If we can maintain our nonviolence, dignity, and sense of humor, serve those in need, take care of ourselves and encourage one another, and, most of all, if we can surrender ourselves fully to the God of Peace and follow the nonviolent Jesus on the road to our own Jerusalems, we can build a global movement of nonviolence and resistance that can push back against all forms of the world's violence. More, we can experience new levels of surrender into God.

After he was arrested for his Plowshares disarmament action in 1980 and faced ten years in prison for hammering on an unarmed nuclear nose cone at the General Electric plant near Philadelphia, Dan Berrigan put it this way: "Simply put, we wanted to taste the resurrection. May I say, we have not been disappointed."

❧

Tuesdays in Guadalupe

As I reflected during the pandemic with my friend Will on these themes of surrender, service, and the political consequences of trying to be led by God, I realized I needed to start serving the poor and disenfranchised. That brought me to my friends Dennis and Tensie, who run Beatitude House, a Catholic Worker house in the village of farmworker families in Guadalupe, California. Through their hard work and with the help of a generous team of supporters, they collect tons of food during the week. Then, every Tuesday morning, they set up tables in the garage, pile the food up, offer prayers, and at 10 a.m. welcome a long line of elderly women and young women with infants, all carrying bags, to take what they need for the week. Each week they distribute tons of food to some two hundred low-income households of farm-worker families, most of them undocumented. They also run a free medical clinic on Thursdays along with free medical and social service advocacy, and on Fridays, distribute free clothing and furniture.

"To be with migrant farmworkers has been an incred-ible journey," Tensie says. "Each of our programs opened up a place of new relationships. Over the years it's been a sacramental experience because we have shared births, baptisms, marriages, and deaths with many, many people. My own understanding of God has deepened and grown within this context of the suffering poor. I've always liked the phrase of Tagore: 'Let the beauty you love be what you do.' It's so important to give our lives to our deepest yearnings, to live them and let them transform you. In my journey with so many people who have no money and few possessions and few privileges, I see how they live only by the grace of God, and they are showing me that we all rely solely on the grace of God every single day to live."

Every Tuesday I drive over to Guadalupe and join friends in the cafeteria-style food distribution. The farmworker families line up, register, and walk along the tables while we place items in their bags. At the end of the line, instead of a cash register, we send them off with a greeting and blessing. Each week we give away rice, beans, potatoes, onions, cereal, pasta, crackers, frozen meats, tuna, lettuce, celery, bread, cakes, and muffins. Their bags are heavy, and everyone is grateful. It's a very happy place.

After several hours, we clean up and load the pickup truck with twenty-five bags filled with food. Dennis and I then drive around town and deliver the bags to those who are not able to leave their homes. At every house we meet an elderly woman and a relative caring for her, or a young mother with a pile of children whose husband is picking strawberries twelve hours a day in the nearby fields. They are always happy to see us.

Guadalupe is surrounded by strawberry fields that seem to go on forever. As I drive by, I see hundreds of Mexican farmworkers bent over in the dirt. I offer a blessing upon them with love that God protect and care for them. Long ago, I spent two memorable weeks working all day in similar fields. I had been house-sitting at the Half Moon Bay Catholic Worker, and it has a program where it takes homeless and low-income people to work in the fields for a meager sum and a beautiful lunch. I worked too, bent over double all day, picking vegetables, washing them, and packaging them. It was the most exhausting work I have ever done in my life.

Dennis, Tensie, and their friends are trying to live out Dorothy Day's method of practicing the works of mercy as described in Matthew 25: "Whatever you did to the least of these, you did to me." One day I pressed Tensie on her connection with God and this holy work of service, especially in light of "surrender."

"When I think of surrender to God, I think of my place in this relationship with God," she began. "It's realizing I have been given this gift of life and how do I want to respond to this gift. It means keeping my ego in check and all my plans and leaving them all to God. Life isn't about earning praise for ourselves or self-flagellation, but responding daily to God, to life, to Jesus in every person and situation. There I find God.

"When I don't surrender, I feel stress, anger, impatience, and doubt. Conversely, when I surrender, when I'm in right relationship with God, then I'm sustained. The negatives aren't driving me anymore.

"We serve the Beatitude people. Jesus said my life is dedicated to the poor, the meek, the hungry, the merciful, the pure, the peacemakers, the persecuted. Over time, I recognize not only the poverty in the world but the poverty in me. I no longer serve others as if they're different. We're all in total need for God. This need for God is both personal and universal, and that's what I'm learning."

From the day I walked into the Beatitude House garage, I have experienced great inner peace and consolation. Every time I have handed out food to someone in need, my own worries, anxieties, and concerns fall away and I look into the smiling face of someone in need. This work of mercy brings with it a rare kind of grace that I cannot find anywhere else. I am the one being served, or better, we are all serving each other. Better still, the grace of God is being poured out upon each one of us. As I get to know the other volunteers and those on the line, and show up each week, I feel the barnacles on my stony, selfish heart being chipped away by God, and I breathe easier. There, on the food line, these humble farmworkers, our lovely neighbors, offer me freedom from my first-world, upper-class entitlement and privilege. They bring the blessing. I hope to keep on returning and learn how, like Dennis and Tensie, to share and receive these Beatitude gifts of peace. Blessing upon blessing.

The End of the World in Haiti

"Love in action is a harsh and dreadful thing compared to love in dreams," Dostoyevsky wrote. This was Dorothy Day's favorite quotation. She knew well that "harsh and dreadful love in action," having lived with and served homeless people for nearly fifty years at the New York Catholic Worker.

St. Francis knew that "harsh and dreadful love in action," too. He made the difficult journey from the life of privilege into the pain of poverty and serving the poor, but he was determined to walk in the footsteps of the nonviolent Jesus, who said, "Take up your cross daily and follow me." So, Francis left the world of comfort and riches and entered the world of the poor and suffering. He let his heart be broken and grew in compassion, selfless service, and universal love. He allowed God to use him to heal many, form community, make peace and in the process, rebuild the church.

In his memoir, *The Cross of Love, the Pain of Poverty,* my friend Gerry Straub shares his roller-coaster journey from the world of Beverly Hills and Hollywood, where he was the producer of the leading soap opera "General Hospital," into the world of the poor to "put the power of film at the service of the poor." Few people in history have had the experiences Gerry has had—traveling into the worst slums on the planet to shed light on the poorest of the poor.

Perhaps it was inevitable that Gerry would one day leave it all behind, move to Port-au-Prince, Haiti, take in a few orphaned children and start a large children's orphanage, all with no money, named Santa Chiara Children's Center. I met Gerry Straub at a book convention in Chicago sometime in 2000. We immediately started talking about books, life, God, Jesus, St. Francis, peacemaking, serving the poor, universal love, and how to help change the world. Twenty-five years later, we're still talking, and the conversation hasn't changed. But Gerry has. He is no longer writing about how he visited the poor and filmed the poor; now he talks and writes about life with the poor in Haiti. His gospel journey of downward mobility has led him to give up everything, live like family among the poorest of the poor, and take up what he calls "the cross of love."

At the time I met Gerry, he was promoting his award-winning book, *The Sun and the Moon over Assisi*. He was just beginning to make films about poverty, to bring the reality of global poverty front and center to North Americans. I was moved and impressed, and I saw at once what he was trying to do: to help us comfortable rich people open our eyes to the suffering of billions of sisters and brothers around the world. The hope and prayer were that we might drop our selfishness and spend our lives serving those in need and working to end poverty.

Gerry was breaking new ground. He was no longer filming a boring afternoon soap opera; this was life-and-death reality for the majority of human beings on the planet. As he witnessed firsthand, and showed us in his films, most people on the planet who wake up alive in the morning don't know if they will have the resources to survive the day. They do not know if they will have any food. This is the reality of poverty, "an early and unjust death," as Ignacio Ellacuría, the Jesuit martyred in El Salvador in 1989, named it.

Through his films, books, and his memoir, Gerry shows us what nobody wants to see, and says what nobody wants to hear. He became "a voice for the voiceless," as St. Oscar Romero put it. And his message is right out of the Gospels: "Blessed are the poor. The kingdom of God is theirs. If you want to follow Jesus, give away your money and your possessions, take up the cross of love and follow. Whatever you do—or do not do—to the least of these sisters and brothers, you do to Christ."

Over the years, Gerry sent me his films, his books, his daily journal, and his latest adventures. I joined his board and tried my best to support his project. He never had any money, but he had a single-minded, stubborn devotion and faith that led him to try to do the impossible. Time and time again he showed us that the impossible was doable and achievable. When he moved to Port-au-Prince, he took in an orphaned girl named Baby. Immediately, other homeless children showed up, and before he knew it, he was housing, feeding, healing, and teaching some seventy children, and hiring many other Haitians to serve with him. He has saved many lives, but as he will tell you, they are saving him. Really, they are all experiencing the palpable grace of God to survive another day in Haiti.

There is little comfort for him in this journey, however, because poverty, as Gandhi said, "is the worst form of violence," so this is a journey into grief, pain and sorrow. That's what it feels like to take up the cross of love. For Haiti and the poor, life is one long Good Friday, one long Holy Saturday. Gerry stepped into that Good Friday world and, like John and Mary, who stood by the crucified Jesus, he now stands by the crucified peoples to love them in all their pain and sorrow.

"For me, Haiti became a school of life," Gerry writes. That is the key to understanding his journey. Gerry is a searcher, one who tries to surrender his life and will to the will of God. He's seeking the God of life and the fullness of life. After a lifelong search that began in the darkness of Beverly Hills and Hollywood, he announces, he has found his "school of life."

Most North Americans would consider Haiti "a school of death." It has some of the worst poverty on the planet and sits like Lazarus on the doorstep of the United States, the richest nation on the planet. Haiti's poverty, like the starvation and wars of Sudan, the US-funded Israeli genocide in Gaza, and the US bombings of Iraq and Afghanistan, cannot be grasped by our blind eyes, narrow minds, and cold hearts, so we turn away. Worse, it is covered up, ignored, and forgotten by the culture of death. We would much rather look at images of the rich and famous. The 2010 earthquake, the hurricanes, the political coups, the military takeovers, the never-ending grinding poverty, the tears of a sick child found in a garbage dump—who can bear such pain? Why bother looking? What difference can one person make? Where is God anyway?

But Gerry speaks of life in the midst of suffering and death, and not just survival, but even the laughter, gratitude, and joy of the children of Santa Chiara. If you take Gerry at his word, you realize that we have every-thing backward: the United States is really the "school of death." We are stuck in the rat-race of making money, buying things we don't need, hoarding possessions, thinking only of ourselves, no longer knowing our neigh-bors or ourselves, and in the process, rushing toward the brink of nuclear annihilation, permanent warfare, and catastrophic climate change—and losing our souls in the process. We are all well schooled in death, yet we presume we've got it all. We're number one! We're the top of the heap. What's your problem? Love it or leave it.

Not so fast. If we take St. Francis—and Gerry—at their word, we've got it all wrong. St. Francis said the only way, in the end, to understand the gospel of Jesus is to stand on your head because everything Jesus does and says is "upside down." The first will be last, the last will be first, the hungry will be fed, the rich will be sent away empty. And the poor will hear the good news: poverty, injustice and war are not the will of God!

I decided to see for myself. So in 2019 I made the long trek to Port-au-Prince. Walking into Santa Chiara, I was mobbed by scores of singing, laughing, happy children. They hugged me and welcomed me like one of the Beatles. It was like that till the moment I left.

All at once, I had stepped into their "school of life." It was as if right there, in the midst of Haiti's charnel ground, a Phoenix rose, a light shone out of the darkness. The children and I played nonstop the entire week. Yes, there was pain and death on every side in Haiti, but because of the cross of love, there was life, and even— dare I say?—the fullness of life. I was changed by that week. For the first time in a long time, there among the poorest of the poor, I felt happy.

The cross of love summons us to live a new kind of selfless service toward those who have nothing, who cannot repay us. From now on, we have not even a trace of the desire for reciprocation. In the process, in this school of life, as we carry the cross of love, we begin to learn.

What are we learning? We are learning what it means to be human, what it means to love and care and show compassion, what it means to follow Jesus. Martin Luther King, Jr., said over and over that "unearned suffering love is redemptive." This is how we let the light shine, how we make peace in our poor world, how we do God's will instead of our own selfish will. All we have to do is share in the paschal mystery of the nonviolent Jesus.

Gerry Straub's mythic pilgrimage is one we can all make, one that Jesus and St. Francis invite us all to undertake in our own particular circumstances. If you dare to drop everything, take up the cross of love, surrender to God's will, and follow the risen, nonviolent Jesus, like St. Francis and Gerry Straub, into the world of the poor in selfless service, steadfast compassion, and universal love, we will taste the resurrection. We, too, will hear the good news: death does not get the last word. Life and love will one day overcome. That's the promise of the gospel. Even in Haiti.

৩০

Gandhi's Dream

In the one hundred volumes of Gandhi's letters, essays, and writings, I found only one prayer that he wrote. It was at the request of a Mrs. Linsforth, who ran a community center in Hyderabad that served Hindus, Muslims, and Christians. She wanted something from Gandhi to strengthen her for her grinding work of unconditional service. He enclosed the prayer in a letter to their mutual friend Mary Barr on September 12, 1934. I included the prayer in my book *Mohandas Gandhi: Esstial Writings*:

> Lord of humility, dwelling in the little pariah
>   hut,
> Help us to search for Thee throughout that
>   fair land
> Watered by the Ganges, Brahmaputra and
>   Jamuna.
> Give us receptiveness, give us open-heart-
>   edness,
> Give us Thy humility, give us the ability and
>   willingness
> To identify ourselves with the masses of
>   India.
> O God, who does help only when we feel
>   utterly humble,

Grant that we may not be isolated from the
    people
But that we would serve as servants and
    friends.
Let us be embodiments of self-sacrifice,
    embodiments of Godliness,
Humility personified, that we may know the
    land and the people better
And love them more.

There it is, right in the middle of the prayer, Gandhi's theology of surrender: God will help us, but only when we feel utterly humble before God. God cannot help us if we think in our delusion that we don't need God, that we have everything under control, that we only need God to do one thing and we can do the rest. Unless we are utterly humble before God, God cannot help us. But if we are utterly humble before God, if we let go of everything, including our lives, and surrender ourselves completely to God and let God run the show, God can help us and does in fact help us, and miracles will occur. Perhaps that's the ultimate prayer: "Not my will, your will be done."

A week before Gandhi's assassination, a journalist asked him what was the greatest lesson he ever learned. "Have nothing to do with power," Gandhi said. "Reduce yourself to zero." Till the very end, as he led India's revolution for freedom from British rule, suffered through the civil war of independence, and repeatedly fasted to the death to end the violence, he practiced total surrender to God, seeking to be utterly humble before God, to claim his powerlessness before God so that God's power could work through him, and save him, and India and the world. This is the lesson of Jesus on the cross, what St. Paul called the "kenosis" of self-emptying, not clinging to God.

Gandhi learned this teaching on surrender from the conclusion of the Bhagavad Gita (18:64–66). The Lord Krishna [God] tells Arjuna [the novice warrior, whom Gandhi understands as a warrior of militant nonviolence], "You are so deeply loved by me, you are my friend." Krishna invites him into complete abandonment which he promises will result in total peace.

This abandonment to God, in all our own spiritual poverty, humility, and powerlessness, was the foundation of Gandhi's spirituality of nonviolence. The key for Gandhi was to reject the world's power, wealth, and glamour, and to choose utter humility before God. He learned from the Gita that God wants to be our friend, that God is wildly in love with us, and that we can unite ourselves to this loving God. He discovered that as he abandoned himself over and over again every day to his loving God and sought to humbly do God's will, he felt a new, private intimacy with God and a sense of deep peace that was out of this world, even as the world's violence swirled around him.

It was from this daily intimate experience of prayerful surrender to God that Gandhi stepped out publicly and built a grassroots movement for justice for the poor and freedom from British rule. Because he had surrendered to God, he was able to remain radically nonviolent and inspire hundreds of millions of people to try to do the same. He wanted everyone to practice "the nonviolence of the brave" and spread the life and politics of faith-based nonviolence around the world. Toward the end of his life, he put it this way: "We have to make truth and nonviolence not matters for mere individual practice but for practice by groups and communities and nations. That at any rate is my dream. I shall live and die in trying to realize it."

Gandhi's dream is still worth pursuing. If groups, communities, religions, and nations seek truth and practice nonviolence with wholehearted love and determination, if more and more of us can surrender ourselves to the God of Peace and try to live as extensions of Universal Love as a people, then nonviolence can become the foundation of every culture, religion, and school, and we will finally begin to welcome God's reign of universal love, compassion, and peace on earth.

༄

The Choice Is Ours

If Archbishop Tutu is right, and God's own universal love and total nonviolence require God to give every human being free will to reject God's plan, and we would like to be Godly people who live in God's peace and love, then each one of us faces a choice, not just once or twice in our lives, not just once or twice a year, but every day, every hour, every minute of our lives from now on.

As Daniel Berrigan put it, we must choose to be chosen.

With every present moment in the life of surrender, we face a new choice. We can choose God's will, God's peace, God's universal love, or not. We can go ahead with whatever random thought comes to our heads, or our selfish plans to make money and control others, or give in to the culture's idolatrous demands of violence, war, and destruction, or go full steam ahead in total surrender to God and let God lead us to do God's will, come what may.

If we surrender ourselves to God, in God's "gracious will and infinite compassion," God may well say to us, "What do you want me to do for you, my beloved?" The answer that we aspire to give from now on is: "Whatever you want to do for me and all of us, beloved God. You decide. You choose. Whatever you want is fine with me."

If we choose each day to let God be God, we will grow in daily conscious awareness of ourselves as extensions of Universal Love, Universal Compassion, and Universal Peace. We will begin a journey of daily inner disarmament and healing that God is undertaking within us, as well as a daily journey of public service that could spread like ripples of universal love and peace around the world, without our even knowing it.

As we deepen into total surrender to the God of Peace, and take steps every present moment to live in harmony with God's desires for the world, we begin to understand that God has a fantastic plan for the human race. We begin to know that God wants to draw every human being into the divine embrace, and we can choose to participate in God's plan if we want to. The choice is ours.

The challenge is to wake from our lethargy, apathy, blindness, selfishness, narcissism, and cultural limitations to surrender to God's universal love and total nonviolence. We do that by choosing God and God's will every day from now on, as we begin our day, as we end our day, as we go through our day, as we live each hour, as we experience each minute. One way to ritualize our solemn surrender to God is to kneel as we first get out of bed in the morning, and kneel as we get into bed at night, and surrender throughout the day and night to God, so that we are constantly giving our hearts, wills, and lives to God.

We notice a change even in the language we use; the focus is no longer "I-Me-Mine," but "You-You-You." We make a change from saying, "I choose to do your will. I choose you God. I choose to be nonviolent, loving, compassionate, just, and peaceful," to "Your will be done. You choose me. You use me and do with me whatever you want since you created me and you know your plan for humanity. You lead me through this moment, this day, this year, this life. You make me an extension of your universal love right now and forever. You do everything. Thank you."

I have learned and witnessed a way to be in this world from many friends, including Daniel and Philip Berrigan, Archbishop Desmond Tutu, Mother Teresa, and Thich Nhat Hanh. They saw pain, suffering, injustice, and death in the most horrific circumstances, but they did not let that crush them. They never let the world's violence and injustice blow out their inner pilot light. On the contrary, they lived according to their inner light, to their conscious and total surrender to the God of Peace, and in doing so, they each knew and experienced an inner joy and peace that came from being used as a channel and extension of God's universal love. I experienced that personally from each one of them, as well as hundreds of other Godly people I have known throughout my life. On good days and bad, even when I forget everything or feel beaten down and discouraged, I remember them and how they transcended the pain and sorrow of the world and dwelt in some mysterious grace and light, and I long to do the same. It is a far better way to live, and a far more useful and fulfilling way to live than drowning in self-will and self-pity.

Only later did I come to see that for each of them peace, love, and gratitude were acts of resistance to the culture of violence. They demonstrated how joy is resistance. So are patience, active compassion, and universal love. Hope in the face of the world's despair is an act of nonviolent resistance. All these graces sustained them for the long haul of surrendering and peacemaking, and they inspired millions. I want to do the same, to live the fullness of peace, hope, love, and nonviolence surrendered to God, and in doing so, to live in full-time resistance to the culture of violence, injustice, and war.

In other words, as they gave themselves to being servants of universal love, peace, and nonviolence, they moved beyond resentment, anger, anxiety, worry, fear, darkness, and despair. They were in a different place from the rest of us. They were trying to change the world, or rather, allowing God to use them to change and disarm the world, and in the process of their total surrender, they were led to an inner liminal place of grief and joy, which is at the heart of God. These friends of God sent out ripples of love, compassion, justice, and peace that continue to travel the ends of the earth.

Surrender, surrender, surrender. That is our new motto, our new mantra, our new path. We let ourselves be people who send out God's waves of energy, ripples of universal love, compassion, nonviolence, and peace wherever we are, wherever we go, whatever happens to us. If we are in the coffee shop, the library, the airport, at home, at work, or in church, we choose to pray for and bless and love everyone around us. We see God in every human being, indeed in every creature and all of creation, and we know that God is everywhere, loving all of us personally, wildly, infinitely.

We choose to live surrendered lives where the God of Universal Love who created us now leads and guides us, whether in our ordinary daily routine or in our public work with the global grassroots movements for justice, disarmament, and environmental sustainability. We know that on our own, we can do nothing. But now we know, too, that if we surrender ourselves right this very moment, and love God, ourselves, and our neighbors with all our hearts, souls, minds, and strength, with our very wills, then anything is possible. This is the promise. We *can* be disarmed and healed. We *can* become nonviolent and kind. We *can* become other-centered, service-oriented, universal people of universal love, compassion, and peace. We *can* abolish war, racism, nuclear weapons, corporate greed, and systemic injustice. We can do all these impossible things because it is no longer us doing it but God, who is using us and our surrendered lives together to disarm and heal humanity and creation.

According to John's Gospel, the day before he was executed by soldiers of the Roman Empire, the nonviolent Jesus told his disciples, "My peace I leave you, my peace I give you. Not as the world gives peace do I give it to you." The world teaches the lie that peace comes about through violence, war, even killing. We are told we can get to peace if we wage war against our enemies. If we kill those who threaten to kill us, if we kill those who kill others to show that killing people is wrong, we will have peace. None of that is true. The nonviolent Jesus spent his whole life practicing and teaching peace through what Gandhi and Dr. King called creative nonviolence and universal love. Jesus was attacked and threatened countless times, until eventually, because of his daring resistance, he was arrested, tortured, and executed. Not once did he give in and respond with violence. He never retaliated. He never even had the desire for retaliation or revenge. He was always steady in peace, truth, and love, as strong and powerful as a mountain. His prayer from beginning to the end was, "Not my will, but your will be done. Into your hands, I commend my spirit."

When he rose from the dead and appeared to his awe-struck disciples on that Easter Sunday night, he told them repeatedly, "Peace be with you." He showed them his wounds, and repeated his greeting, "Peace be with you." In that resurrection moment, he offered a peace that is not of this world. It is the peace that comes about through total surrender, nonviolence, non-retaliation, and unconditional, universal love. If, like the nonviolent Jesus, we choose not to respond to violence with further violence, if we dare respond with love, surrender ourselves to God, and practice creative nonviolence, then, come what may, we will know a new kind of peace.

Life is short. We have only so many years left. Even if we eat right, lose weight, exercise daily, and take care of ourselves, our time on earth is limited. What do we want to do with the time that is given us? How can we get beyond ourselves and help relieve suffering and disarm the world? If we surrender our hearts, wills, and lives to the living God of Peace, I believe we will be given the resurrection gift of peace, and become instruments of God's peace and universal love. Resurrection means having nothing to do with death, having not a trace of violence within us. When we live in the peaceful spirit of resurrection, we find ourselves practicing the boundless love and gentleness modeled for us in the nonviolent Jesus, who came to reconcile humanity to God, which is the ultimate act of peacemaking. This resurrection peace is ours for the asking if we dare choose it and surrender.

If we dare surrender to the God of Universal Love and Peace right now, then we can go forth into the world of violence and war, without fear, worry, anxiety, or anger, and be transforming agents of loving nonviolence like Gandhi and Dr. King, and know, with the medieval mystic Julian of Norwich, that "all will be well, all will be well, all manner of things will be well."

～ゐ

Prayer

God of Universal Love and Peace, send me forth to be an extension of your Universal Love and Peace

> God of Universal Love and Peace,
> Send me forth!
> Make me a true extension of your Universal
>   Love and Peace.
> Let me live fully abandoned to you, surren-
>   dered to you in love, that I may spread
>   your love far and wide, serve and heal
>   those in need, disarm others, seek jus-
>   tice, and pass on your gift of peace.
> Give me strength to rise to the occasion, to
>   serve your global peace and love move-
>   ment for the creation of justice, environ-
>   mental sustainability, and a new culture
>   of nonviolence.
> Do with me what you will, and as I do your
>   will, bring forth your reign of Universal
>   Love and Peace every new every day.
> Amen

Closing Prayer

God of Peace,

May everyone surrender to you, do your will, and welcome your reign of universal peace, love, and nonviolence here on earth.

God of Peace,

Thank you for all the blessings of life, love, and peace that you give us.

Take me and use me that I might do your will today and humbly play my part in your plan to welcome your reign of universal peace, love, justice, and nonviolence here on earth.

Disarm me, heal me, awaken me, inspire me, enlighten me, surrender me to you and send me forth as your humble servant and channel of universal love, peace, and nonviolence that I may be who you

created me to be, your beloved child,
a holy peacemaker living in the light of
your peace from now on, bringing your
peace, love, light, consolation, and joy to
everyone I meet, and all humanity, and
all creation.

May everyone surrender to you, do your
will of peace, love, and nonviolence, and
together, may we all welcome your reign
of universal peace, love, and nonviolence
here on earth, and love you and one
another forever. Thank you. Amen.

Postscript

❧

"But how do I take all this from theory to practice?" Will asks. We're back at the Blackhorse Café, drinking coffee, talking about surrender, service, nonviolence, and the God of Universal Love. It's an ongoing conversation about our ongoing practice.

"Ah!" I say. "What did Universal Love tell you? Did you ask Universal Love?"

He looks at me.

"We have to return to Universal Love each day in our meditation and surrender to Universal Love all over again," I suggest. "I don't think we can put any of this into practice on our own. That's precisely the point. We're helpless and powerless. But if we humbly surrender ourselves to Universal Love every single morning and throughout our day, then over time Universal Love can put it all into practice in our lives. It's the relationship with Universal Love that makes all the difference."

He takes a sip of coffee and thinks about this.

"It sounds easy in theory," he says, "but it's challenging in practice. It's easy to climb Mount Everest while sitting on a sofa and dreaming about it, but when you're doing it, when you are in the midst of an emotionally jarring situation, how do you remain centered, calm, and mindful?" He pauses. "I guess we try, fail, and try again, and that's our practice."

I review the basics: daily meditation, daily surrender to the God of Universal Love and Peace, creating a circle of likeminded friends who love you or even join a community that will support you on your journey to God. Listen to teachers; read Wisdom literature and scriptures; experiment with public service, action, and nonviolent resistance; and live one day at a time in peace, compassion, humility, and love, toward yourself and all others. And experiment. Experiment in the small moments when you feel agitated, disturbed, or unsettled. Surrender all that to God, let God handle it, ask to do God's will and try to do it, and try to be more peaceful.

"But how can you surrender when life is one setback after another?" he asks.

"All you have to do is live in intimate relationship with Universal Love," I tell him, "with the God of Peace. Then, you'll be fine. Life becomes an adventure in surrender, a journey of love, compassion, peace, grief, and joy. You have all the tools you need to respond to every situation because ultimately you are surrendered and living in relationship with Universal Love who really loves you and cares for you and will protect you. All the wisdom teachers say as well that it's best to try to live in the present and not worry about the future or dwell on the past. In the present moment, you can choose to surrender to God, do God's will, and breathe easy that Universal Love has got your back. Indeed, the setbacks fade and you concentrate on your intimate relationship with God, with Universal Love, and all other relationships. As you do, you find yourself at one with Universal Love."

"I feel a physical relief when I surrender," he tells me, as he has told me before.

That sounds right, I respond.

"But how can I make this a way of life?"

"You can't," I say. "You can only choose right now in this moment to surrender to Universal Love, and try to do the will of Universal Love right now, and go forward every moment trusting in Universal Love. Only later, when you look back, will you notice that you are living a whole new way of life, something you could not have planned, something you could not have imagined, something—actually—that you yourself could not have done. Take it from me. The more we let Universal Love run our lives, the better our lives will be, and we will enjoy them more, and go from miracle to miracle as we serve others."

"How can I not be a Neanderthal when I like being a Neanderthal?" he asks.

I speak of the mess we create for ourselves when we act in our Neanderthal nature, when we give in to selfishness, ego, self-seeking, and control; when we let ourselves become werewolves, run wild with the pack, and join the culture of violence, war, and death. In those moments, I tell him, I discover all over again just how helpless and powerless I am on my own. As long as I try to be in control, my life is out of control and I ruin everything and hurt everyone. I'm just a Neanderthal, a werewolf, a zombie, despite my best intentions. So, I turn again in humility to Universal Love and say, "This is awful, I'm a mess, I don't know what I'm doing, I surrender myself to You. You take control. Your will, not mine, be done." Over time, over the years, we begin to see how much better life is when we surrender completely to Universal Love. Our Neanderthal nature may always be there, but we can notice it, be calm about it, and not feed it or let it rule our lives. We let Universal Love rule our lives. You'll be amazed to see how much better, how much more peaceful you can feel over time.

I ask him what he thinks. He takes my note pad and writes a few sentences: "Surrender requires an element of faith, faith that we can let go because something wiser is beyond the mess. Faith is acceptance that we were never behind the wheel to start with, and it's cathartic to realize that and let go and trust and have faith in the One who is driving."

"I believe in a Force of Universal Love that connects all beings," he says. "I surrender to that."

I quote a line from one of Daniel Berrigan's poems: "The outcome is in better hands than ours." And another thing he once said to me: "We only get enough light for the next step."

"I'm realizing it's not a linear process," Will says. Sometimes, I handle things better than I did when I was twenty-three, sometimes worse. It's like climbing a mountain." I can see that he is remembering how he climbed through the deep snow to the top of Mount Whitney last year with his friend. "Each step gets harder. You slip and slide. There is a little dying with each step along the way. But enlightenment awaits at the top."

I know what he means, but I also know it all gets easier the more we let go, surrender, and hand over the reins to Universal Love. What interests me, I tell him, is how we get used, in our surrender to Universal Love, to serve humanity and creation, and thus Universal Love. With Universal Love, not only will we climb mountains, but we will move mountains. Over time, I suggest the wonder, the focus, the joy becomes Universal Love. As we get to know Universal Love over a lifetime, we are filled with childlike wonder, and even in grief we can know a deep contentment and joy. That's why Daniel Berrigan used to wake up, open his eyes to God, and say every morning, "Astonish me!" I think God loved that.

"In the end," Will says, "I guess the question is: Do we want to be better versions of ourselves or not? If the answer is yes, then there are going to be real implications. There are real implications for becoming a better human being," he says. "You end up serving others and creation."

"And you become humble," I add. "You let go, turn to Universal Love, surrender yourself, and along the way, start becoming who you were created to be—an extension of Universal Love. Life has a deep new meaning. There is grief, but there is joy, too. As Daniel Berrigan wrote long ago, the greatest joy is to know that your life serves."

He sips his coffee and nods.

It's time to go, but we know that the conversation, the adventure of surrender to the God of Peace, and the pilgrimage of peace into Universal Love, will continue.

As we go to press, Will has graduated near the top of his class at the leading graduate school for paramedics in the nation. He is now serving full time on the front lines on the streets of Southern California.

Also by John Dear

Disarming the Heart
Our God Is Nonviolent
Seeds of Nonviolence
The God of Peace
The Sacrament of Civil Disobedience
Peace Behind Bars
Jesus the Rebel
The Sound of Listening
Living Peace
Mary of Nazareth, Prophet of Peace
The Questions of Jesus
Transfiguration
You Will Be My Witnesses
A Persistent Peace
Put Down Your Sword
Lazarus Come Forth!
The Nonviolent Life
Thomas Merton Peacemaker
They Will Inherit the Earth
The Beatitudes of Peace
Radical Prayers
Walking the Way
The Gospel of Peace
Praise Be Peace

THE GOSPEL OF PEACE
A Commentary on Matthew, Mark, and Luke
from the Perspective of Nonviolence

JOHN DEAR

In this original and inspiring new commentary, Father John Dear walks us through every line of the three synoptic Gospels, pointing out Jesus' practice and teachings of nonviolence each step of the way.

As Dear shows us, Jesus is nonviolent to the core, a disarming, healing presence toward those in need. The authorities of his time killed him only to push him to the heights of nonviolence through his death and resurrection.

Here is a fresh, new approach to the Gospels for all, sure to inspire everyone most particularly those who preach or engage in social ministries in these troubled times.

PRAISE FOR *The Gospel of Peace*

"[This] detailed look at how the synoptic Gospels emphasize nonviolence is a sorely needed contribution in a country and a church that blur the stark lines between Christianity and militarism."
—*America*

"*The Gospel of Peace* lovingly confronts us all with what it means to follow Jesus in all dimensions of life. It is a master class on Christian discipleship."
—**The Rt. Rev. Mariann Edgar Budde, Bishop, Episcopal Diocese of Washington, DC**

"Belongs in the hands of every priest and deacon, every minister and chaplain, and every politician and leader in our country (and the world)."
—**Herman Sutter,** *Catholic Library World*

"John Dear's is a beautiful message of peace!"
—*Anne Lamott, author, Traveling Mercies and*
Almost Everything

Catholic Media Association Award Winner
First Place—Life and Dignity of the Human Person

The Association of Catholic Publishers Award
Second Place—Scripture

440pp., scripture index, paperback
ISBN 978-1-62698-533-9

ORBIS BOOKS
A Ministry of Maryknoll Fathers and Brothers

From your bookseller or direct: OrbisBooks.com
Call toll free 1-800-258-5838 M-F 8-4 Eastern